Deconstructing Energy Law and Policy

Deconstructing Energy Law and Policy

The Case of Nuclear Energy

Raphael J. Heffron

EDINBURGH
University Press

Edinburgh University Press Ltd
The Tun – Holyrood Road
12 (2f) Jackson's Entry
Edinburgh EH8 8PJ
www.euppublishing.com

Typeset in 11/13pt Monotype Baskerville by
Servis Filmsetting Ltd, Stockport, Cheshire,
and printed and bound in Great Britain by
CPI Group (UK) Ltd, Croydon CR0 4YY

A CIP record for this book is available from the British Library

ISBN 978 0 7486 9666 6 (hardback)
ISBN 978 0 7486 9668 0 (paperback)
ISBN 978 0 7486 9667 3 (webready PDF)
ISBN 978 0 7486 9669 7 (epub)

Contents

Tables

Figures

Acknowledgements

During my research for this book I had the opportunity to attend many presentations and meet many wonderful academics, and I thank the University of Cambridge, the Judge Business School, the Energy Policy Research Group, Massachusetts Institute of Technology, the University of Texas at Austin, the British Institute of International and Comparative Law and other institutions for these experiences.

I expressly thank Professor William Nuttall and Professor Angus Johnston from whom I have learned so much about academic life, careers and research. In particular I thank them both for their guidance, direction and support throughout this project.

I would also like to convey thanks to all those who agreed to be interviewed for my research and all those administrative staff who helped coordinate such meetings.

Sincere thanks also go to my family for their assistance and understanding. And finally, this book is:

Le haghaidh mo bhean chéile agus mo h-oileán.

CHAPTER 1

Introduction

In contemporary societies in the modern world, *energy law and policy* has increased in importance. It now plays a crucial component in the functioning of the economy. Countries have international obligations with which to comply and these influence their own national policies. Energy law and policy represents in part the response of a government to some of these international treaties, driven by a battle against climate change. The struggle to contain climate change is one of the greatest challenges of this era and is an area that needs significant further research (Giddens 2009).

Many countries, however, currently struggle to have effective energy policy that will deliver the low-carbon energy infrastructure needed to reduce carbon dioxide emissions. This book focuses on the development and formulation of energy law and policy. The aim is to ascertain what are the constituent parts of an energy law and policy by deconstructing its current form. In achieving this, the aspiration is to enable the improved delivery of the goals of energy law and policy. This book's focus on one of the most complex energy sources is intended to increase understanding of the *raison d'être* of energy law and policy. Consequently, the case study at the core of this book is the provision of civil nuclear energy.

Nuclear power has, since its emergence as an electricity source after the Second World War, been a consideration and part of the energy policies of many countries across the world. Nuclear energy is a low-carbon energy source and therefore can contribute to reducing the effects of climate change. For this reason alone it is an area that requires further attention by scholars (Giddens 2009; Helm 2007; Keay 2007; MacKay 2009).

There are several additional reasons for further research in the area, which include, principally: the risk associated with nuclear power (Ash 2010); the high initial cost of nuclear and its economic viability (Joskow 2006; IAEA 2008); and the long timeframe for nuclear plant operation and waste disposal (Chapman and McKinley

1987; IAEA 2008). These issues of risk, high cost and waste apply also to other energy sources.

Apprehension over the security of electricity supplies has also placed nuclear energy back on the agenda of governments. During the post-Second World War period, concerns over the security of supply dominated energy policy. These were resolved through public ownership and statutory monopoly. However, many have advocated that it was precisely these solutions that led to security of supply problems (Helm 2007).[1] Hence, competition was encouraged and, in the 1980s and 1990s, energy was treated as just another commodity. However, energy policy has been re-politicised and now, since 2000, security of supply concerns dominate all international fora including G8 and European Union (EU) summits (Giddens 2009; Helm 2007). This is because energy policy has in part become foreign policy, as a result of the Middle East and Russia owning some 90 per cent of oil reserves (Stevens 2007). Energy security has even become a NATO mission, although this organisation was originally established for militaristic purposes.[2] Further, it is debatable whether competition policy and the liberalisation policy for energy markets have delivered the hoped-for results.

Within energy policy is nuclear energy policy, which suffers from even more complexity in the political, economic and legal spheres (Ash 2010). Energy policy has, however, always been political (Giddens 2009). If not centred on State-owned companies and security of supply concerns, the political focus was on introducing competition, and now energy policy focuses on all three of the aforementioned issues. MacKerron (2004) states that nuclear energy is special (as a technology and therefore as an energy source) and unlike other (ordinary) energy sources, and he argues that if it were to achieve an 'ordinary status' it would be a more popular option. Part of this special status emanates from nuclear power also being used for militaristic purposes, and hence more control over its use is needed to prevent nuclear weapons proliferation.

In examining nuclear energy – and in this book the development of new nuclear energy infrastructure – one has to understand its complexity. It is highly politicised in terms of EU energy policy[3] and holds a special status. It is significant that nuclear energy is controlled by the EU under a separate legal instrument in the form of the Euratom

Treaty, created in 1957 alongside the other EC treaties that formed what is now the EU. Nuclear energy policy is dominated by a myriad of political, economic, legal and environmental issues.

Research methods and case selection

Interviews were at the core of this research with ninety-six interviews completed across Romania, the United States and the United Kingdom (for more information on the interviewees, see the Appendix). Four tiers of actor groups were identified, as shown in Table 1.1. Interviews were conducted in the three countries from September 2009 to June 2012. Interviewees lasted between twenty and 120 minutes, with an average interview time of sixty to seventy-five minutes. Over 90 per cent of the interviews were conducted in person, and all of the interviews that were recorded were done so with the permission of the interviewee.

Table 1.1 Stakeholders identified and interviewed: UK research example

Interview reference code	Category name	Function, organisation*
1	State institutions/ public sector	DECC Office for Nuclear Development, Office for Nuclear Regulation, Nuclear Decommissioning Authority, Environmental Agency, European Commission, Euratom
2	Industry private sector	Westinghouse, EDF, Eversheds, Atkins, 39 Essex Street Chambers, MottMcDonald
3	Academic researchers	Oxford Energy Institute, Cambridge Nuclear Energy Centre, Lancaster University, University of Greenwich, Warwick University, University of Manchester, Cranfield University
4	NGOs	Nuclear Industry Association, World Nuclear Association, Independent Nuclear Researchers, Chatham House

*For full list see Appendix.

Elite actor group interviews in the nuclear energy policy literature are rare. This research therefore offers a new categorisation class (see Table 1.1) of the various actor groups in nuclear energy policy literature that will be instrumental for consistency in further research in the area. Previous studies that incorporate elite interviews in surrounding areas have not categorised the interviewed stakeholders owing to the low number of interviews performed.

Elite interviews have the added benefit of providing immense amounts of information not available in official published documents or other published sources (Lilleker 2003). The interviews conducted were semi-structured interviews and these have been described as a useful research method for revealing the motivations and perceptions of respondents (Flick 2002). Aberbach and Rockman (2002) state that: 'interviewing is often important if one needs to know what a set of people think, or how they interpret an event or series of events, or what they have done or are planning to do'.

Owing to the different backgrounds of the respondents, it was judged to be unsuitable and too constraining to standardise interviews. Instead, the aforementioned flexible 'semi-structured' approach was used (Burnham et al. 2004). An interview guide with a (prioritised) earlier list of topics and hypotheses was used to steer the discussion, although the order in which the questions were asked and their precise wording was not determined in advance in some cases (Devine 1995).

In the interviews, interviewees were asked to focus on the period 1990–2012. This was achieved by asking them what were the major developments in the nuclear sector over that period of time. The interviewer then proceeded through a list of hypotheses derived from prior research and elicited the response of the interviewee to these hypotheses by making a statement and/or question and asking the interviewee his/her opinion. In other cases, the interviewee stated his/her view on the issues without the need for intervention. The interviews followed a semi-structured approach based around ten to twelve hypotheses. Hypotheses were asked as statements in order to gather each interviewee's opinion but were deliberate statements, and no attempt was made to lead the interviewee in a certain direction. This method is known as *Legal Formulation Analysis*, which involves primarily *contested and uncontested hypotheses analysis*. In the analysis that follows in each chapter, only the hypotheses where there was not a majority of 75 per cent in agreement are fully analysed, for reasons which are explained below.

There are three main legal characteristics of the methodology. The *first* is that it is fundamentally adversarial and incremental in its approach to the analysis of the data – in this case the contrasting viewpoints from the expert interviews. The research hypotheses are debated with the interviewees who state (or it is elicited from them) whether they are proponents or critics of the hypothesis. The method is similar to the US Environmental Protection Agency (EPA) methodology of *Expert Elicitation* (see US EPA 2011 and earlier 2009 draft); however, it is noted (2011: 68) that Expert Elicitation is a financially expensive methodology, and hence the methodology used here is more suitable for a single researcher.

The research method is useful where an affirmative or negative policy action occurs – i.e. whether or not a nuclear power plant is to be built. In this scenario, a majority is needed and the majority figure of 75 per cent is chosen. Only hypotheses that are contested by interviewees to a sufficient degree (where there is no 75 per cent majority of interviewees in favour or against) are further analysed. Those that are uncontested are research results in themselves – in that there is consensus on those issues – and these are not discussed in as much depth.

The *second* legal characteristic of the methodology concerns the choice of the figure of 75 per cent. In civil court trials a verdict can be reached with ten out of twelve jurors in agreement or nine out of ten (Juries Act 1974 s. 17). The threshold of 75 per cent chosen here reflects that, but is adjusted lower, and thus is less severe, since it is policy-related decisions that are under analysis rather than actual court proceedings; nevertheless the aim is to secure a high majority who are in favour of or against the policy action. The method aims to achieve a consensus view similar to the aim of an environmental planning enquiry.

The results established are based on the experts' (those interviewed) knowledge and understanding of the policy and legislative issues. Similar to the aforementioned Expert Elicitation methodology of the US EPA, the contributions of this research can be thought of as: (1) a description of the state of knowledge, and what we know and do not know; (2) a process by which we obtain better information (to reduce primarily uncertainty); and (3) both (1) and (2) improve the understanding of existing observations (US EPA 2011: 28).

The *third* legal characteristic begins by aiming to determine whether the hypotheses are proven or unproven. This decision is based on in-depth interview analyses (coded and analysed), analysis of policy actions and documents (including those suggested by interviewees), and further literature review. The decision on whether the hypotheses are proven or unproven is similar to a judge making a judgment/decision in a civil trial on the balance of probabilities. The researcher (being the judge) will then on the balance of probabilities declare each hypothesis proven or unproven.

The empirical data in this research was analysed using coding categories that were developed from the literature review that reflected the key issues in nuclear new build, and five key issues were identified: (1) legal and policy development, (2) public administration, (3) project management, (4) economics of nuclear energy, and (5) safety and education. The data was sorted, and further subcategories developed. The advantage of such a qualitative data analysis is that it allows for statements and claims of various interviewees to be corroborated against other interviewees. This is also a validity process that is of central importance to qualitative research (Miles and Huberman 1994).

A key concern of the study was to safeguard its research validity. Hence, an extensive process of primary qualitative analysis – in the form of elite interviews, legal texts, official documents and industry reports – was supplemented by secondary qualitative analysis. This adheres to the principle of triangulation, which 'entails using more than one method or source of data in the study of social phenomena' (Bryman 2004: 275). Findings from secondary analysis could thus be verified by outputs from semi-structured interviews. A case study methodological approach permits triangulation and makes the results more robust and valid (White 2000).

Overview

This work builds on other in-depth studies on nuclear new build: see Jasper (1990); Hecht (1998, 2009); Pope (2008), and the Royal

Academy of Engineering (2010). In particular, the approach of this research is similar to Jasper (1990) who conducted a study with over 100 stakeholder interviews in examining nuclear energy policy. His focus was also on three countries (the US, France and Sweden) from the time of the 1970s oil crisis to circa 1990. His interviews included managers, policymakers and activists in the three countries. More recently, the Royal Academy of Engineering in the UK (2010) completed a report on nuclear new build based on interviews with key stakeholders in the area focusing on *lessons learned*. Indeed, that interviews have begun to emerge as a dominant data source in nuclear new build studies is evidence of the need to garner more understanding of the complex policy analysis required to illustrate the issues in question. Other studies on nuclear energy policy also use interviews: see Stoler (1985); Morone and Woodhouse (1989); and Perin (2005). It is notable that these latter studies and others – Goodman and Andes (1985); Campbell (1988); Nohrstedt (2008); Royal Academy of Engineering (2010) – draw *lessons* from their assessment of nuclear energy policy, a similar objective to this research.

This book has three main parts. The first part includes two chapters. Chapter 2 examines the key elements of a nuclear energy policy. It emphasises the interdisciplinary nature of energy law and policy, and also identifies a clear distinction in terms of which issues are *country-specific*, and which are *international*. Chapter 3 then gives a brief overview of the two regions, the European Union (EU) and the United States (US), that form part of the later analysis. The aim of Chapter 3 is to show how energy law and policy in the EU (with the UK as an example) and the US is characterised by being quite ineffective and taking a long time to deliver new energy infrastructure – the purpose for which it has been introduced in the majority of cases.

The second part of this book focuses on the country analysis and includes two chapters on the US and two on the EU (the United Kingdom and Romania). The book, in deconstructing energy law and policy, covers in general the time period from 1990 to 2012 with reference to a limited number of events prior to 1989 and post 2012. As the text evolves from Chapter 4 to Chapter 7, the book aims to deconstruct with more clarity the component parts of energy law and policy. By Chapter 7, it has become clear which are the key parts of energy law and policy, and how to improve policy delivery in the energy sector.

Chapter 4 on Romania examines the progress of Romanian nuclear new build amidst the turbulence that the country has experienced during the twentieth and early twenty-first centuries. Romania's transition from communism to democracy during the 1990s was won with bloodshed, unlike the peaceful revolutions across much of the rest of Central and Eastern Europe. The transition period has not been without controversy, and there still remain question marks over the operation of some of the Romanian democratic institutional structures. Nevertheless, despite the political, economic and social upheaval in Romania, the country has successfully established a nuclear power programme. The research on Romania highlights many lessons for emerging civil nuclear energy nations about the problems, issues and considerations that they will have to address in order to develop a safe and operational nuclear energy plant on time and on budget.

In determining what energy law and policy consists of in the US, there are two main focuses. First, Chapter 5 examines from a policy perspective US Federal policy inaction and contradiction in the nuclear energy sector from 1990 to 2010. This chapter, as befits policy research, engages with many disciplines (in particular, law and politics), and hence the debate moves beyond nuclear energy policy and also includes, in particular, discussion of law and policy issues for other large infrastructure projects. Secondly, Chapter 6 examines nuclear energy policy across three states in the US – Georgia, Pennsylvania and Texas – from 1990 to 2010. The research provides new insights through a unique comparison of US states that have deregulated, regulated and 'hybrid' electricity markets. From the research it is evident that law can have a central role in the nuclear energy sector, and that policy in the nuclear energy sector can become state-driven. The chapter also considers the impact of public administration and legal development in developing new nuclear energy policy.

Chapter 7 focuses on planned nuclear new build in the United Kingdom. As the nuclear energy programme process begins again in the UK, the research focuses on five key issues in the nuclear new build process: (1) law, policy and development; (2) public administration; (3) project management; (4) the economics of nuclear; and (5) safety and education. If the UK is to achieve a sustainable nuclear energy policy, these issues are of major importance. Further, the research identifies that policy in the area remains to be resolved, in particular at an institutional and legal level. However, contrary to the literature in some areas, the research identifies a change of course as the UK concentrates on delivering a long-term policy for the nuclear energy sector and the overall energy sector.

The final part of the book provides its conclusions. In Chapter 8, energy law and policy are fully deconstructed and the components parts used to form an energy strategy. This energy strategy is advanced using a nuclear energy strategy as an example. Then the key points are summarised about deconstructing energy law and policy, and future research issues are identified as energy policy deadlines and goals approach for 2020, 2030 and 2050.

CHAPTER 2

The Different Dimensions of Nuclear Energy Policy

Accidents and calamities . . . are the universal legislators of the world.
(Plato 1975: 164)

2.1 Introduction

There are many elements of energy law and policy and this chapter begins with a preliminary identification of these. This is is achieved by exploring how nuclear energy law and policy is examined in research. A review of the evidence demonstrates the range of issues, from accidents and safety to finance and energy security. A list of the majority of component parts of an energy policy are detailed before being narrowed down in the discussion in later chapters.

The two major accidents at Three Mile Island (US) and Chernobyl (Ukraine),[1] in 1979 and 1986 respectively, stalled new nuclear energy infrastructure in Europe and North America. However, with the approach of the year 2000, nuclear power began to be recognised for its potential to curtail climate change due to its very low emission levels of carbon dioxide, and consequently nuclear energy returned to the policy agenda; by some this has been mooted as a 'nuclear renaissance'. However, on 11 March 2011 a nuclear incident occurred at Fukushima in Japan which has slowed down this potential nuclear renaissance. The full effect of this disaster has yet to be ascertained and will only be clear perhaps a decade after it occurred. Nevertheless, the disaster has resulted in an increase in research on the consequences of major energy accidents. In this context, it draws many comparisons with the BP Deepwater Horizon oil spill disaster in the US on 20 April 2010.

2.2   The interdisciplinary nature of nuclear energy policy literature

Recent studies into nuclear energy policy have called for more research in the area. For example, the IAEA (2008) has expressed the need for more studies to be completed in nuclear energy policy, highlighting the need for country-specific studies. Similarly, Pope (2008) states that the nuclear sector is in need of more research, particularly on nuclear new build processes and policy.

Research in nuclear energy policy has several certain notable characteristics. There is a strong focus on the major accidents at two nuclear power stations,[2] namely Three Mile Island and Chernobyl. Research is also very country-specific and mainly focused on Western countries.[3] International research also concentrates on distinct issues such as nuclear new build, the success and failure of nuclear projects, licensing, safety, public attitudes, or a combination of all of these. In the country-specific literature the focus is on one country or, in rare cases, two or more countries. The case study on nuclear energy presented in this book has a major emphasis on the nuclear build process, which is rare in the nuclear energy policy literature. In addition, in a similar way to other books on nuclear energy, this book incorporates data from interviews (Jasper 1990; Hecht 1998, 2009; Tweena 2006; Pope 2008; Nuttall 2010; Baker and Stoker 2011).

The literature coverage for nuclear energy policy is interdisciplinary and extensive, as is demonstrated in Figure 2.1. The figure shows classifications for the various issues that the literature covers in nuclear energy policy (which is represented by the core yellow circle), although these are not stringent classifications. The second circle highlights that a paper will concern one of the disciplines of law, politics and/or economics (the yellow circles that navigate the core), or will involve the interaction of all three. The third circle is where the characteristics of nuclear energy policy literature are evident (with the blue boxes identifying the three central characteristics: nuclear renaissance, country-specific and nuclear new build) and in general a paper can be identified as having one or more of these characteristics. Then the rest of the grey shaded area identifies more specific areas of research, with white boxes signifying these specific classifications.

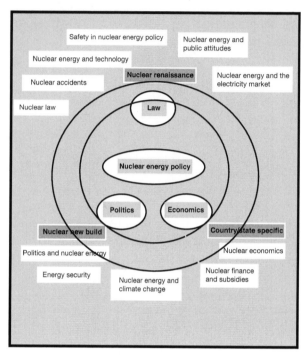

Source: Compiled by the author from the Academic Literature Survey in 2008–12

Figure 2.1 Classification of nuclear energy policy academic literature

Research in nuclear energy policy not only covers the classification (topic) at the core of a paper, but will cross into many of the other classifications (topics). For example, a paper on nuclear law may incorporate safety, technology, engineering, economics and politics issues. This is evident in the way that published research articles on nuclear energy policy are not confined to a few select journals, but appear in philosophy, sociology, psychology, law, economics, management, science, engineering and physics journals.

In general, an academic paper in nuclear energy will cover three or more of the classifications outlined in Figure 2.1. Hence, it is evident that a paper on nuclear energy policy will, in general, combine at some level a mix of law, politics and economics. Some will combine all three, in particular the literature that deals with nuclear new build, country/state-specific analysis and the nuclear renaissance.

Over the past decade, climate change has also become an issue in nuclear energy policy. This is because of the current international agenda to reduce CO_2 emissions across the world. Nuclear energy is viewed in many countries as a clean energy source and thus, if included in the energy mix, will lead to lower carbon emissions. Consequently, literature on climate change and nuclear energy policy demonstrates how one article covers several of the nuclear energy policy literature classifications (in Figure 2.1). For example, Sailor et al. (2000) state that nuclear energy can be a solution to climate change. However, in their article they also cover other topics such as nuclear economics, nuclear waste disposal and nuclear proliferation.

2.3 Specific examples of research in nuclear energy policy

It is evident from examining research in nuclear energy policy that the core areas are nuclear economics, nuclear law, risk, political economy, and electricity policy; examples of these are examined in more detail below. Additionally, a range of other topics is detailed, though these are not as relevant as those mentioned above; examples of these are utility rate regulation (Drobak 1985); nuclear energy technology and learning effects (Zimmerman 1982); nuclear weapons as a reasonable cost for peace (Waltz 1990); nuclear new build and proliferation (Harding 2007; Aherne 2011) nuclear energy and public attitudes (Drottz-Sjoberg and Sjoberg 1990; Kitschelt 1986; Joppke 1991; Rosa and Dunlap 1994; Gamson and Modigliani 1989); nuclear safety (Feinstein 1989); and risk sharing and nuclear fuel (De Roo and Parsons 2011).

2.3.1 Nuclear law literature

Law is always at the forefront of nuclear energy policy. This is because, in particular, it is from the law that three major policy issues emanate: safety legislation; legal complexity; and the operation of the courtroom in hearings on nuclear energy.

In general, the main sources of nuclear law are from international standards and guidance documents. In nuclear law the concept of safety is paramount. Safety is the primary requisite for the use of nuclear energy and the applications of ionising radiation (Stoiber et al.

2003). This is necessary as continued safety success in the sector secures its future, particularly in terms of the high investment needed for new nuclear facilities and research activities. The safety concept therefore has to be emphasised in national laws and regulations, international agreements and treaties, and all other policy reports and documents produced on nuclear power. This is achieved through several principles that relate to safety being integrated into the aforementioned legal and policy instruments on nuclear. These principles are:

1. The prevention principle – holds that the primary objective of nuclear law is to prevent damage that may be caused by the use of nuclear technology, and to minimise any adverse effects from an accident or its misuse;
2. The protection principle – states that the purpose of a regulatory regime for nuclear is to balance the social risks and benefits from it. Priority must be given to protecting public health, safety, security, and the environment where the risks associated with a nuclear activity outweigh the benefits – or a balance cannot be achieved; and
3. The precautionary principle – this holds that in respect to the previous principle in decision making on nuclear the concept of preventing foreseeable harm should be prevalent (Stoiber et al. 2003).

In the formulation process of law in the nuclear sector, the hierarchy of risk of nuclear issues operates. A fundamental set of safety principles should apply in the broadest manner, with stringent and strict principles on safety where activities pose a risk to the public particularly in terms of radiation risk. Nevertheless regulations should not impose undue limitations on a person or firm; this latter issue is a constant point of debate in international nuclear law formulation (Tonhauser and Wetherall 2010). Of note is the advocation that safety is of paramount importance in nuclear law and in its formulation. This is of particular importance due to the increased number of countries that have no nuclear facilities and intend to build civil nuclear power. Bouquet (2003) examines this issue of growth in the nuclear industry from a legal perspective in an article focusing on the EU entitled 'How Current are Euratom Provisions on Nuclear

Supply and Ownership in View of the European Union's Enlargement?' The author concludes that Euratom supply provisions are still quite current and relevant for new EU entrants; however, significantly he states that '[T]hey normally should not generate problems' (Bouquet 2003: 38).

Nuclear law also examines the protection of the citizen through nuclear safety regulation. This has been the focus of much research at a national level (Cavers 1964; Helman 1968). However, of significance has been the rare focus on legislation introduced at US state level in terms of what individual states were enacting to ensure differing levels of safety. Parenteau (1976) writes that in the 1970s, various states (Vermont, Iowa, Oregon and California) enacted legislation that went further than Federal legislation in terms of health and safety regulation. This highlights the action of states in comparison to Federal action in the case of nuclear energy.

A further issue in nuclear energy law is the examination of its complexity as a subject matter. Breyer (1978) notes the complexity of nuclear energy and concedes that in many cases the law courts lack sufficient expertise and should, in their rulings and decision-making processes, defer to the judgement of existing nuclear energy and other governmental agencies. In contrast, Yellin (1981) advocates the creation of new agencies, while Cameron (2007) states that serious attention needs to be given to legal change in light of a nuclear revival. Yellin (1981) proposes the creation of a permanent review board, composed of experts trained in science and law, to which technological and scientific issues falling outside the special competence of the judiciary would be referred by the Federal appellate courts. Furthermore, Yellin (1981) notes the complexity of civil nuclear development issues and the failure of nuclear regulation, and states that the procedural requirements of the adversarial system tend to impede full presentation of the issues in nuclear law cases and demonstrate the need for a new system to review nuclear legal cases. The lack of expertise in the courtroom on nuclear energy issues demonstrates the need for hybrid legal and scientific oversight of technological decisions and thus the creation of the new aforementioned agency. In contrast, Maleson (1982) argues that the courts have been only too willing to concede to the expertise of agencies, citing the tension between the humanities and sciences as to why legislation for public safety and protection has not been further researched nor reforms considered.

2.3.2 Nuclear economics

There is a considered view, which emanates from the assessment of the economics of nuclear power, that nuclear energy is an unattractive option in comparison to other energy sources. The main reason for this is the oft-cited long construction times for nuclear power plants (Cantor and Hewlett 1988; Mooz 1978, 1979; Paik and Schriver 1979; Komanoff 1981; Zimmerman 1982; Applied Decision Analysis 1983; Navarro 1988). Navarro (1988) identifies three major reasons why nuclear energy is not economical in many countries – stating that the other countries could not attain the same industry performance levels as Japan. A nuclear plant is built twice as quickly, at half the cost, and runs at a higher average capacity factor in Japan. Other costs to a nuclear project emanate from a variety of other factors. There are costs associated with the delay in legal processes and particularly in planning applications (Cantor and Hewlett 1988). Others point to the cost of the nuclear fuel cycle and in particular, the part concerning high-level radioactive waste (Proops 2001).

Research on nuclear economics also concerns itself with projected costs. Authors state that the nuclear industry receives too many subsidies: such as in the US through the Price Anderson Act (Dubin and Rothwell 1990). An early article in this regard by Joskow and Baughman (1976) examined the future of the nuclear industry for the next twenty years, from the 1970s onwards. They stated that demand for nuclear would be affected by the costs of air pollution control affecting coal utilisation, the costs of uranium and uranium enrichment, the price of oil, and electric utility regulatory practices. Notably, they predicted that the pace of the continued evolution of the nuclear industry would slow down. Further, a Massachusetts Institute of Technology report (2003, 2009) states that although in general all costs will be lower for future nuclear new build projects in the US, nuclear power remains more expensive than gas or coal – it states in many of the outcomes calculated that gas will be up to 45 per cent cheaper, with coal being up to 35 per cent cheaper.

Despite this view that the economics of nuclear energy are unattractive, there is an alternative view that the economics of nuclear energy are more than favourable when other issue are considered. Aherne (2011) states that obstacles to future nuclear new build go beyond the economic cost issue and encompass public attitudes, nuclear waste and workforce shortages. The positive changing nature of public attitudes towards nuclear energy is also well documented (in the US, Greenberg 2009; in the UK, Pidgeon et al. 2008; Goodfellow et al. 2011), while the nuclear waste issues remain a problem that governments have yet to resolve – as is identified in the subsequent chapters on the US and EU. Skills and expertise shortage issues in the sector are also a central issue.

Nevertheless, other authors assert that some contributions of nuclear energy are unquantifiable such as, for example, its contribution to the energy mix and consequently to energy security. Rossin and Reick (1978) state that nuclear energy diversifies the supply of electricity in many states and overall in the US. This is of benefit to the US and its population for energy security reasons (Rossin and Reick 1978). Similar assumptions have been advanced in the UK by Watson and Scott (2010), who state the importance of nuclear energy for energy security.

2.3.3 The political economy of nuclear energy

Clarke (1985) debunked the view that it was through the military that the commercial nuclear industry grew in the USA. He stated that the military did not benefit from the commercial nuclear industry, and that the industry developed because the government forced utilities to develop nuclear. Interestingly in Clarke's research (similar to the research methodology behind this book), he ignored the consensus view of those who gave testimony to the US Congress concerning nuclear energy: i.e. where there was uniformity despite the type of person testifying (utility executives, politicians and scientists). Instead, Clarke (1985) examined the testimony of those utility executives, politicians and scientists who were unprepared, and the answers to questions after formal statements had been given.

Clarke's research concluded that the decisions for the development of the nuclear industry were political and not economic, and that nuclear energy is a complex policy topic. Hultman (2011) too states the importance of political decision-making in the development of the nuclear sector and cites three main reasons for this: (1) climate change issues; (2) regional employment; and (3) the need for govern-ments to retain a military nuclear capability; though this last issue is not applicable to all countries, in particular to those that had or have no prior military nuclear capability before embarking on a nuclear programme.

Hohenemser et al. (1977) state that nuclear power is in trouble. They pre-date the 1979 Three Mile Island accident and hence the conclusions reached are interesting in that context. They state that nuclear energy is assessed by the public more critically than other energy sources for three fundamental reasons: (1) its unique history and complexity, (2) the underestimation of regulatory tasks and safety management, and (3) the 'rancorous nature of the debate' (1977: 43). The conclusions of Weinberg (1972), Director of the Oak Ridge National Laboratory in the US, are similar in this regard, in that he stated that a problem for nuclear energy is social institutions. Nuclear energy, in comparison to other energy sources, offers clean energy: however, the issue of waste disposal requires those with the highest levels of expertise to be involved in nuclear energy, and the social institutions responsible for nuclear energy do not have the longevity of existence to help protect the public.

Rothman and Lichter (1987) in examining nuclear energy policy look at elite ideology and risk perception. They hold that it was in the 1960s that the public began to demand more of a role in shaping policy – influenced by the emerging environmental movements in the 1960s and 1970s. They state that journalists and the media are responsible for the inaccurate portrayal of scientists' views on nuclear energy. A key conclusion from Rothman and Lichter's (1987) research, which is relevant here, is their identification of a mistrust of authori-ties, and conflict within elite leadership groups, both of which hinder the growth of the nuclear energy sector. This follows from an earlier assertion of Temples (1980), who states that the nuclear power indus-try is like a sub-government in itself, and that the industry is domi-nated by this sub-government elite. Further, this issue is demonstrated with the government-established company Nirex Limited (Nuclear Industry Radioactive Waste Executive) in the UK and its deep disposal plans for nuclear waste in the 1980s. The UK government had a stated policy of being committed to transparency and to facili-tating trust and understanding and acceptance of government policy;

however, in practice, Nirex did not develop the repository near
Sellafield mainly due to its approach to securing approval for the
Deep Waste Repository, which demonstrated a clear lack of transparency, in particular with the local Cumbrian community (Hetherington
1998).

2.3.4   Electricity policy

Joskow (2005) reviews the electricity markets of the US and concludes
that well designed competitive market reforms have benefited customers through lower retail prices. Nevertheless, Joskow (2005) states
that the transition to competitive electricity markets was a difficult
process. His main concern before the process was started was whether
policy-makers would implement the reforms effectively, and significantly this remains a concern (Joskow 1997; 2005). Further, Joskow
(2005) identifies that electricity policy is an imperfect subject and
consequently he expects to see both forms of State electricity systems
survive – regulated and deregulated electricity markets.

In this regard, Slocum (2008) criticises the view that electricity
deregulation has been a success in the US. He deems it a failure, with
consumers suffering not only from an increase in prices but also from
more power being given to the Federal Energy Regulatory Commission
(FERC), which does not have consumer interests on its agenda.
Further, he argues that the government at the Federal level is pushing
competition while some states such as Illinois, Michigan and Virginia
have all moved to re-regulate since 2007. Joskow (2005) had highlighted that there were problems in the wholesale market, and Slocum
(2008) identifies these and states that the problems in the wholesale
market have meant that consumers do not really have a choice in
retail prices: only 10 per cent of consumers have a choice. Slocum
advocates an extensive reform of deregulated electricity markets.

Blumsack (2007) has also examined the restructuring process, and
states that it is unclear whether electricity deregulation in the USA
has been a success or failure. Notably he states that there is a lack of
clarity or long-term policy integrated into the electricity market
regime (Blumsack 2007: 183–4). This is similar to findings in Europe
from Thomas (2010) and Kennedy (2007). Further, Blumsack (2007)
identifies a problem which is also a key aim of this book and that is
how can society assess whether policy goals have been met.

2.3.5 Nuclear risk

Risk for nuclear energy is viewed primarily as technical risk; however, social, economic, political and legal risks are also explored in relation to risk and nuclear energy. Nelkin (1981) writes on the social and political dimensions of nuclear power, and demonstrated that the accident at Three Mile Island highlighted the difficulties in assessing social risks from such a technology, and the political difficulties in managing these risks; this, he states, emphasises the need for policy research in the area. Palfreman (2006) identifies three risks in the nuclear sector as he explores the relationship between the media and nuclear power: (1) risk assessment – the skills needed by nuclear policy-makers to measure the likelihood and consequences of adverse events; (2) risk perception – the ability to understand how human beings think about those events; and (3) risk communication – the ability to tell a story effectively.

Palfreman (2006), quoting from Nelkin, states the problem is that the public understands science 'less through direct experience or past education than through the filter of journalistic language and imagery' (Nelkin 1995: 2–3), and that therefore public policies (and the fortunes of the public) are linked to the practice of journalism for complex policy issues. In this regard, Kuklinski et al. (1982) examine how citizens choose one policy over another, and whether informed citizens make their choice using a different method to those who are uninformed. Knowledgeable citizens draw heavily on ideology which colours their cost-benefit risk calculations (at the variable levels that they make this calculation), while the unknowledgeable draw on their generalised outlook on technology and the cues of the various groups involved in the nuclear energy controversy.

Kasperson et al. (1980) analyse risk in a broader context and state that in the US the prospects for nuclear energy depend on a variety of factors: the success of energy conservation, the long-term competitiveness of nuclear energy, the growth of coal production, the future 'Three Mile Islands' in the US or internationally, and the changing regulatory environment. However, for Kasperson et al. (1980) the key risk concerning nuclear energy is the risk of whether the nuclear industry can gain society's consensus to sustain nuclear new build programmes. This revolves around whether the benefits of nuclear power outweigh the risks (the so-called Faustian bargain) and whether they are worth these risks.

Similarly, the EU now requires Member States to go through a 'Justification Process' for new reactor designs (European Council Directive 96/29/Euratom of 13 May 1996). Furthermore, Kasperson et al. (1980) predict a slow pace of attitude change on nuclear. However, of important relevance to this book is their observation that US states and cities have – and need to play – a more active role in nuclear policy-making. In this context, Goodfellow et al. (2011) discuss the management of risk perception in the nuclear industry, and they call for more stakeholder input in the design of nuclear power programmes – in effect, to develop further consensus across society on nuclear energy.

2.3.6 Policy crisis, shocks and contradictions in nuclear energy policy

Nuclear energy policy can also be examined in terms of policy crisis, shocks and contradictions. Goodman and Andes (1985) assess the politics of regulatory reform within nuclear energy policy. This is from the perspective of the policy crisis and contradictions that occurred in nuclear energy policy in the US prior to and following the accident at Three Mile Island. From the lessons drawn in their assessment, Goodman and Andes advocate a new approach, but do not develop it. Campbell (1988) focuses similarly on nuclear energy policy in the US and its contradictions, though fails to assert how the lessons learned can be applied in future scenarios.

Morone and Woodhouse (1989) explore the lessons for the control of nuclear technology under the rhetorical question of whether nuclear energy was experiencing demise or not. Their work assesses the view that the non-democratic control of technology in the nuclear sector was influential in the decline that nuclear energy experienced in the late 1980s. Notably, they identify similar lessons to those of Pope (2008) who focuses on Washington State in the US. Norhrstedt (2008) conducted similar research in establishing what has been learnt from Sweden's approach to nuclear energy policy after Chernobyl. Crisis in policy-making guides the identification of these lessons. This book aims to go one step further by focusing on the exploration of successful policy; there is a difference between exploring energy policy which is ongoing and that which has been successful in terms of bringing a new energy infrastructure into operation.

2.4 Conclusion

There is other research on nuclear energy. However, again much of it is pre-Chernobyl and pre-Three Mile Island, while later research in the area is more focused on energy policy in general rather than nuclear energy specifically (see below for examples).

Kitschelt (1982) advocates the benefit of and need for comparative research in nuclear energy policy. This research complies with this view with its focus on the US and the EU. Wison (2000) states that public policy tends to go through long phases of stability before abrupt episodes of substantial change. Bruggink and van der Zwaan (2002) highlight the recent change in energy policy and note the role that nuclear energy can play, while emphasising that there will be new structures to which the sector will have to adhere. They advocate that more research should be completed to establish and identify these new structures and their consequences. Ash (2010) examines nuclear energy policy with a focus on risk assessment for nuclear energy; however, he notably stresses the legal, political and economic complexity of policy for the nuclear energy sector. Accordingly, this book aims to explore these three themes from Wison (2000), Bruggink and van der Zwaan (2002), and Ash (2010) in the context of the change that has occurred in policy for different phases of new build nuclear projects, and hence to demonstrate what are the effective parts of nuclear energy law and policy.

Overall, it is evident that research on nuclear energy policy is country-specific or internationally focused. This research combines these two factors but is more country-specific than international, with a focus on Romania, the US and the UK. This chapter assesses the research literature on nuclear energy policy to demonstrate the distinct parts of energy law and policy in relation to nuclear energy. It is clear that economics, law and politics form the core of the research concerning nuclear energy policy. The following chapters chart a course to see whether these core areas can be deconstructed further. The question asked is what are the fundamental parts of energy law and policy that ensure a policy is not only formulated and brought into being but also delivers results.

CHAPTER 3

An Overview of EU and US Energy Legislation

3.1 Introduction

Legislation in the energy sector is in the process of change across the world. A common characteristic is the length of time it takes to formulate new energy law, for it to be applied and for it to deliver. This chapter discusses this in relation to the development of energy law that aims to initiate new nuclear energy infrastructure. The aim is to show how energy law and policy in the EU (with the UK as an example) and the US is characterised by being ineffective and, most significantly, taking a long time to deliver new energy infrastructure, the purpose for which energy law and policy has been introduced in the majority of cases.

In comparison to the EU and many of its Member States, the US is more advanced in the development of its energy law and policy, having introduced major legislation in the area in 2005. Nevertheless, energy law and policy in the EU and US is characterised by 'delay', so that it takes a long time to deliver what the law and policy set out to achieve. It is possible to identify in US energy legislation four areas where the problem of delay may arise. These are: the length of time it takes for incentive schemes to be become operational; the regulatory agency; policy inaction over a nuclear waste management programme; and the 'test case' delays that can be expected.

The EU and Member States such as the UK can learn from these drivers of delay for an energy project and introduce mechanisms to resolve these issues. For example, the UK has spent a long time developing its energy legislation; late in 2013 it introduced, through the UK Energy Act 2013, its own list of incentives, and also reformed in part the regulatory regime (in terms of agencies). There still remains the issue of whether the UK suffers from too many policies rather than policy inaction and it has its own 'test case' for the new legal regime with Hinkley Point C.

The US case highlights the prospect of potential delays in what was its test case with a nuclear energy project. The development of Plant Vogtle in Georgia may take a total of thirteen years to become operational. This amount of time is from the introduction of energy legislation designed to incentivise new nuclear energy infrastructure to the first nuclear reactor coming into operation. Hinkley Point C seems certain to be the test case for the new UK legal regime, its equivalent of Plant Vogtle. If so, and as will be demonstrated later in this chapter, it is conceivable that Hinkley Point will not be brought into operation before 2026 at the earliest.

3.2   Energy law and policy development in the US

The centrepiece of nuclear legislation in the US is the Atomic Energy Act of 1954 (42 USC 2011 et seq.) which is a comprehensive Federal statute that regulates possession and use of radioactive material and facilities that produce or use such material. There are also several other statutes that cover more specific aspects of the regulation of radioactive material and facilities, for example, in radiological protection, radiological waste management, non-proliferation, exports and nuclear security.

Key laws in the nuclear energy sector are:

• Energy Reorganisation Act of 1974: the Atomic Energy Commission (AEC) was abolished and the Nuclear Regulatory Commission created, with other functions going to what later became the Department of Energy.
• Department of Energy Organisation Act of 1977: this combined several government energy agencies together to form the Department of Energy (DOE). The DOE then became responsible for the development and production of nuclear weapons, the promotion of nuclear energy and other energy-related work.
• The Energy Policy Act of 2005: this encourages the development of nuclear power specifically, with several forms of incentives introduced. These take the form of loan guarantees, carbon-free production tax credits, protection tax credits, and a new form of risk insurance for the first six reactors. The aim of the legislation

is to move the US towards a national goal of energy independence with the aid of nuclear power. It also continued the Price-Anderson Act.

• Price-Anderson Act of 1957: this has been revised several times, by updates to section 170 of the Atomic Energy Act 1954, and more recently by the Energy Policy Act of 2005. The purpose of the act is to provide a Federal compensation fund of $10 billion should there be a nuclear accident. The Act does limit liability and does not guarantee payment should possible funds be exhausted already.

The recent law, the Energy Policy of Act 2005 (hereafter also referred to as the '2005 Act') has been significant for nuclear energy in terms of the incentives it has offered but has not yet delivered any nuclear new build. Indeed, only one state, Georgia, has benefited from the loan guarantees system. Overall, despite the surge of eighteen applications to build new nuclear projects after the 2005 Act, it was only in 2011 that the first company (Southern Nuclear from Georgia) was awarded loan guarantees under the Act. Further, the amount available under the loan guarantee system has been demonstrated to be significantly low. This is because the 2005 Act allowed for $18.5 billion for loan guarantees, with the Georgia project claiming nearly 50 per cent ($8.33 billion) of these. Hence, only two projects will be able to use the loan guarantee system. Efforts have been made to increase the amount but these have failed: the Obama administration debated and unsuccessfully sought an increase of up to $36 billion in 2010 (Chu 2010) and $54.5 billion in 2011 (Holt 2011). Other incentives offered under the 2005 Act are outlined in Table 3.1.

3.2.1   The improvement of the Nuclear Regulatory Commission (NRC)

The Nuclear Regulatory Commission (NRC) has improved as an institution over the 1990–2010 period since its previous existence in the 1960s and 1970s as the Atomic Energy Commission (AEC). The NRC was conceptualised as an independent regulatory agency which replaced the AEC in 1974. The late 1970s and 1980s were a very tough period for nuclear energy in the US due to the oil crisis and a financial crisis, and the nuclear energy sector was also subject to a period of continuous regulatory change.

Table 3.1 Selection of incentives from the Energy Policy Act of 2005

Issue	Incentive offered
Construction risk (s. 638)	Offers risk assurance to cover 100 per cent of delays (up to $500 million) for the first two nuclear plants and 50 per cent of delays (up to $250 million) for plants three to six.
Insurance (Title VI, Subtitle A)	Extends the Price-Anderson Act that applies to the civil nuclear energy sector for a further twenty years.
Loan guarantee system (Title XVII)	Creation of new loan guarantee office for any clean energy technologies. Authorises loan guarantee (up to 80 per cent of project cost for nuclear) but also for IGCC (Integrated gasification combined cycle) plants and renewable energy projects, hydrogen fuel cell technology, carbon capture and sequestration projects, and the construction of refineries for gasoline, ethanol and biodiesel.
Production tax credits (s. 1306)	Production tax credit 1.8 cents per kilowatt-hour for 6,000 megawatts of capacity from nuclear power plants for the first eight years of operation. Wind and closed loop biomass have received a production tax credit since 1992 and received a further extension of this (s. 1301 for federal land projects).
Permit process (s. 365)	Permitting process for oil and gas was streamlined and this cuts out years and months of delays in a Western states pilot programme – it will bring new gas and oil to the market sooner. Section 366 even states it is possible for a permit to drill to be issued within thirty days – though this is for a pilot project across Western states only.

Source: Compiled by the author in October 2011 from NRC statistics (2011)

The NRC in the late 1980s aimed to address the concerns regarding, and the lessons learned from, the licensing of the 104 plants that were operating in the US. This involved the revision of the entire system and the introduction of a new one – the Combined Operating and Licensing system (COL). This new licensing system was designed to minimise delays in the process of awarding licenses, and also aimed to standardise design applications. Of significance is the fact that no licence has yet been granted under the new COL system. The Plant Vogtle project in Georgia will be the first to go through the new legal regime, and will be the test case. After the test case the NRC can improve upon the lengthiness of its licensing process and hence approval times for nuclear reactors will decrease.

3.2.2 Policy inaction over nuclear waste management

Policy inaction is evident in the nuclear waste management policy of the US and it remains unresolved. There is widespread agreement that one of the major obstacles to a nuclear revival is the management and storage of spent nuclear reactor fuel and other high-level radioactive waste. According to the literature, the nuclear industry has concentrated and solved many of its problems; however, it has not resolved this one. Indeed, the conclusions of Weinberg (1972), former Director of the Oak Ridge National Laboratory, still resonate today. He stated that a problem for nuclear energy is social institutions. Nuclear energy in comparison to other energy sources offers clean energy; however, it has a waste disposal issue that requires the people with the highest-level expertise to be involved in nuclear energy, and this knowledge is not retained in social institutions over time (Weinberg 1972).

The US Federal government assumed the responsibility of dealing with the disposal of high-level radioactive waste. This was due to take the form of a long-term deep underground geological depository storage facility and its location was to be at Yucca Mountain in Nevada. However, no state welcomed the idea of being a nuclear waste ground, despite the existence of a small high-level nuclear waste facility in New Mexico for the military (Moore 2011). Indeed, Moore (2011) calls for states to take an increased role in the nuclear waste issue due to Federal indecision on the matter. Public opposition is high in Nevada, though a fraction of the population in Nevada is in favour of it for the economic benefit of having the facility in their state. Senator Harry Reid (Nevada), as Senate leader, was responsible for ensuring that the vote never came before the Senate, as an election loomed and a new Senate was formed. However, other locations are expected to be considered in time as the Blue Ribbon Commission reported (2012) on its examination of the nuclear fuel and waste issue in the US. Nevertheless, the US Federal government has been slow to examine alternatives, or to resolve and fund research into alternatives, though the debate on nuclear fuel recycling is growing.

3.3   Developments in UK energy law and policy

Policy at a national level in UK in the energy sector has been in a transitional phase (see Table 3.2). Consistency has not been at the forefront of policy development. The many White Papers have often been conflicting and government policy towards nuclear energy only emerged in 2008 with the White Paper on Nuclear Power (Department for Business Enterprise and Regulatory Reform 2008). Since privatisation emerged as government policy, the electricity sector has been subject to constant tweaks and revisions.

Whether the policy of privatisation has been a success is debateable. However, what is clear is that strategies for investing in the

Table 3.2 Policy and legal development in the electricity sector

White Papers and legislation, 2002–11

2002	The Energy Review
2003	Energy White Paper: Our Energy Future – Creating a Low Carbon Economy
2006	The Energy Challenge: Energy Review Report 2006
2007	Meeting the Energy Challenge: White Paper on Energy
2007	Planning for a Sustainable Future White Paper
2008	Meeting the Energy Challenge: A White Paper on Nuclear Power
2008	Energy Act chapter 32
2008	Climate Change Act chapter 27
2008	Planning Act chapter 29
2011	Planning Our Electric Future: A White Paper for Secure, Affordable and Low-carbon Electricity

future of the electricity market seem to have been neglected. This is one of the reasons why Chris Huhne, then Secretary of State for Energy and Climate Change, stated in his Foreword to the 2011 White Paper Planning Our Electric Future that, 'Keeping the lights on will mean raising a record amount of investment. However, the current market arrangements will not deliver investment at the scale and the pace that we need' (Department of Energy and Climate Change 2011a: 3). Indeed, in the same note there is an acknowledgement to the failure of privatisation as a policy in terms of the future development of the electricity sector: 'Since the market was privatised in the 1980s the system has worked: delivering secure and affordable electricity for the UK. But it cannot meet the challenges of the future' (2011a: 3).

3.3.1 Legal change: the UK planning process

Nuclear energy in the UK has a history of long planning processes for nuclear new build. Indeed, the Sizewell B inquiry spanned six years, 1981–7 (it was the last nuclear power plant built in the UK). However, the Planning Act 2008 (hereafter referred to as 'the Act') has sought to rectify the problem of long planning processes. Quite what was the driver for the creation of the Planning Act is unclear. It is evident, however, that it applies to all Nationally Significant Infrastructure Projects (NSIP), which are defined as sixteen different categories and include electricity generation (Part 3, s. 14). However, there are limiting factors, and in order to be considered an NSIP a new electricity generating unit must have, when constructed or extended, a capacity of 50MW if onshore and 100MW if offshore. The Act does not distinguish between different types of generators. Nevertheless, the net result for a nuclear energy project is that it is defined as a NSIP since a new nuclear project will be over the 50MW threshold. Hence, the Act's objectives will all apply to new nuclear energy projects.

To say that nuclear energy development was a key driver for the creation of the Act is not to consider three other major issues which were key drivers in themselves. These three major issues are Heathrow Terminal 5, the White Paper on Nuclear Power 2008, and the Planning Bill 2007–8. Heathrow Terminal 5 was a £4.2 billion project that was finished in 2008; however, it had endured a lengthy nearly seven years (Department for Communities and Local Government 2007) – and very public planning process (Doherty 2008). The White Paper on Nuclear Power (Department for Business Enterprise and Regulatory Reform 2008) marked a major change in the then government's energy policy and it detailed the different aspects of the nuclear energy sector, but its main conclusion was that:

> The Government believes new nuclear power stations should have a role to play in this country's future energy mix alongside other lowcarbon sources; that it would be in the public interest to allow energy companies the option of investing in new nuclear power stations; and that the Government should take active steps to facilitate this. (2008: 7)

This strong focus on nuclear energy was further supplemented by the Planning Act 2008, which had at its core the Planning Bill 2007–8 (this in turn emanated from the White Paper 2007 Planning for a Sustainable Future) and two papers that encouraged the change: the Barker Review of Land Use Planning (2006) and the Eddington Transport Study (2006). All these three documents advocated change to decrease the length of the planning process for reasons described as economic and inhibiting the development of other policy goals (for example, on climate change).

The key provision of the Planning Act 2008 was the introduction of a new system for approving major infrastructure projects of national importance. The objective was to streamline these decisions and avoid long public inquiries (with an estimated saving of £300 million a year). This new regime meant decisions are taken by an independent Infrastructure Planning Commission (IPC), the members of which are unelected, and which base decisions on national policy statements (NPS). The hearing and decision-making processes are rigidly bound to a timetable. The Act even specifically states that the system will be used for energy developments such as large-scale renewable projects, and for nuclear power.

The literature on the issue of large infrastructure projects (or, as called in the Act, NSIPs) and planning is sparse. However, this should be expected as the system based around NPSs and the IPC is as yet untested in the courts and remains open to debate. Further, the Coalition government of 2010 had its own ambitions to reverse some of the legal changes of the Act, though this has not yet happened (see Open Source Planning: Green Paper 2010 Policy Green Paper No. 14 (Conservative Party 2010)). The literature in the area that does exist points towards three recurrent themes:

1. While the planning system needed to be reformed to reduce the length of the process, this should not occur if the due process of law is not upheld (Robinson 2009; Grekos 2010; Clarke and Cummins 2011).
2. Law in the area will have to be reviewed once other connecting policy goals are established (Commons Energy and Climate Change Committee 2011; Bircham, Dyson and Bell 2009).
3. Legislating for the unknown, and proactive legislation (Robinson 2009; Commons Energy and Climate Change Committee 2011).

3.4   An assessment of delay as a result of new energy law in the US and UK

In the UK context, it is important to examine policy and legislation development in the US. In 2005 the US introduced legislation that arguably favoured nuclear energy. Yet it was not until 2012, seven years later, that the first nuclear project was given full permission to begin construction. However, a time period of six years is expected for the reactor to be built and put in operation; hence it will be 2018 when the reactor comes online. This means that, since the introduction of the Energy Policy Act of 2005 it will be thirteen years before the first nuclear reactor comes into operation. This timeline is demonstrated in Figure 3.1.

If the UK were to experience a delay of a similar nature, and factoring into account that the 2011 White Paper Planning Our Electric Future only became law in part through the Energy Act 2013, then the next nuclear reactor (Hinkley Point C) is arguably thirteen years away from operation. The UK expectation for its next nuclear reactor coming into operation would be in 2026, as shown in Figure 3.2. This prompts the question: are there lessons from the US experience?

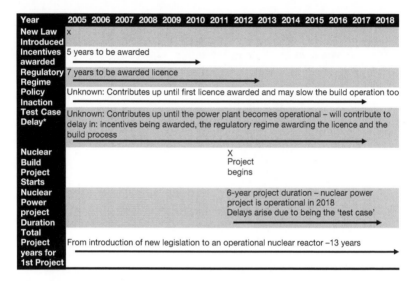

Year	2005	2006	2007	2008	2009	2010	2011	2012	2013	2014	2015	2016	2017	2018
New Law Introduced	x													
Incentives awarded	5 years to be awarded →												
Regulatory Regime	7 years to be awarded licence →												
Policy Inaction	Unknown: Contributes up until first licence awarded and may slow the build operation too													
Test Case Delay*	Unknown: Contributes up until the power plant becomes operational – will contribute to delay in: incentives being awarded, the regulatory regime awarding the licence and the build process →												
Nuclear Build Project Starts								X Project begins						
Nuclear Power project Duration								6-year project duration – nuclear power project is operational in 2018 Delays arise due to being the 'test case' →					
Total Project years for 1st Project	From introduction of new legislation to an operational nuclear reactor –13 years →												

*Test Case Delay refers to the delay associated with the first project to use the new technology and to test the new legal regime for approval, construction and eventual operation.

Source: Compiled by the author based on data from the NRC (2011), Southern Nuclear (2011)

Figure 3.1 Concurrent contributors to delay in a nuclear energy project: the US example

3.5   Conclusion

The development of law in the energy sector in the US provides interesting lessons for the UK. This is the case in particular in the electricity sector in relation to nuclear energy. In the UK, legislation for the electricity sector is currently undergoing a transformation, and new law was finally introduced in 2013 after the publication of the 2011 White Paper Planning Our Electric Future. The reason for this, according to the White Paper, is that within the next decade a quarter (around 20 GW) of existing generation capacity will be lost and needs to be replaced to avoid any potential 'costly blackouts' (Planning Our Electric Future 2011: 5). This will require a suggested a £110 billion investment by 2020 and this is more than double the current rate of investment (2011: 6).

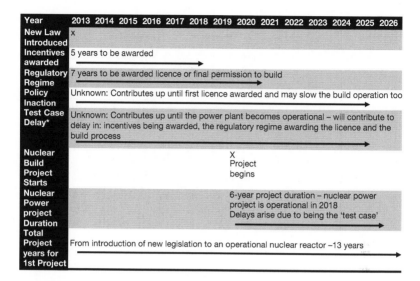

Year	2013	2014	2015	2016	2017	2018	2019	2020	2021	2022	2023	2024	2025	2026
New Law Introduced	x													
Incentives awarded	5 years to be awarded													
Regulatory Regime	7 years to be awarded licence or final permission to build													
Policy Inaction		Unknown: Contributes up until first licence awarded and may slow the build operation too												
Test Case Delay*		Unknown: Contributes up until the power plant becomes operational – will contribute to delay in: incentives being awarded, the regulatory regime awarding the licence and the build process												
Nuclear Build Project Starts									X Project begins					
Nuclear Power project Duration									6-year project duration – nuclear power project is operational in 2018 Delays arise due to being the 'test case'					
Total Project years for 1st Project		From introduction of new legislation to an operational nuclear reactor –13 years												

*Test Case Delay refers to the delay associated with the first project to use the new technology and to test the new legal regime for approval, construction and eventual operation. Southern Nuclear anticipates a four-year construction period for both reactors at Plant Vogtle – this chapter states that because this is first of its kind technology and because of a new regime, there will be a two-year delay.

Source: Compiled by the author based on data from the NRC (2011), Southern Nuclear (2011)

Figure 3.2 A preliminary prediction of delay in a UK nuclear energy project based on US assumptions (see Figure 3.1)

The US introduced a major piece of legislation in 2005 called the Energy Policy Act of 2005. Yet, this Act in relation to nuclear energy finally witnessed many of its component parts being applied at the beginning of 2012. This is seven years after its introduction. If the same scenario were to apply in the UK, the anticipated investment needed in the electricity sector by the government will take considerably longer to materialise than is expected by all stakeholders in the energy sector. In the case of nuclear energy, the earliest project may not be ready to be connected to the grid until circa 2026.

It is clear that the effectiveness of energy law and policy needs to be examined. One of the main ambitions of energy law and policy is to develop new energy infrastructure; currently it seems this process is mired by 'delay' across the US and EU, and in many other countries worldwide. The constituent parts of energy law and policy need to be identified, and a focus placed on each individual part to ensure it is functioning successfully. This can contribute to increasing the effectiveness overall of energy law and policy, and its ability to deliver new energy infrastructure. The following chapters aim to break down and deconstruct energy law and policy so that its individual parts can be identified. This culminates in combining them into a strategy in order to advance a better method of achieving effective energy law and policy that delivers new energy infrastructure.

CHAPTER 4

The Development of Romanian Nuclear Energy Law, 1990–2010

4.1 Introduction

Romania's transition from communism to democracy during the 1990s was won with bloodshed, unlike the more peaceful revolutions across much of the rest of Central and Eastern Europe. The transition period has not been without controversy, and there still remain question marks over the operation of some of the Romanian democratic institutional structures. Still, despite the political, economic and social upheaval in Romania, it has successfully established a nuclear power programme. Although the pace of construction has been very slow, nevertheless it has two reactors with good safety records and ambitious plans to further develop its nuclear power programme. The chapter demonstrates key aspects of Romania's energy policy that have led to a relatively successful nuclear energy policy. It enables the beginning of the assessment of the key components of an effective energy policy that continues in the later chapters. In addition, as the number of countries that plan to build nuclear power plants increases, Romania provides an example of what can be achieved despite political, legal and financial challenges.

The focus on Romania and the development of a civil nuclear programme at a time when the country had limited financial resources, political transformation and limited legal structures is timely. It demonstrates that less developed countries can develop their own civil nuclear energy, and this can be achieved with safety and non-proliferation as core values. This chapter provides lessons for other aspiring nations as listed in Table 4.1 – some of which suffer from political, social and economic turbulence – on how to build operational civil nuclear power capacity.

A focus on Romania is important from a number of other perspectives. Previous studies on nuclear energy policy are very country-specific – which is outlined later in the chapter – and there is a need

Table 4.1 Emerging civilian nuclear countries

World zone	Countries
Europe	Albania, Serbia, Croatia, Portugal, Norway, Poland, Belarus, Estonia, Latvia, Turkey
Middle East and Africa	UAE, Saudi Arabia, Qatar, Kuwait, Yemen, Israel, Syria, Jordan, Egypt, Tunisia, Libya, Algeria, Morocco, Sudan
Africa	Nigeria, Ghana, Senegal, Kenya, Uganda, Namibia
South America	Chile, Ecuador, Venezuela
Central and Southern Asia	Azerbaijan, Georgia, Kazakhstan, Mongolia, Bangladesh, Sri Lanka
South East Asia	Indonesia, Philippines, Vietnam, Thailand, Malaysia, Singapore, Australia, New Zealand

Source: Compiled by the author from World Nuclear Association and IAEA statistics, as of November 2010

to broaden research with new case studies. There is also little research conducted on Romanian and Eastern European countries in general. Of more significance, however, is that Romania is the last European country to bring a nuclear power plant into operation; it is the only EU country that uses Canadian nuclear energy technology (CANDU).

4.2   A history of Romania: politics, geopolitics, energy policy and nuclear power

4.2.1   Romania: a brief history

> God has turned his face toward Romania again. (Statement by Mircea Dinescu, poet and former dissident, who was first to speak on liberated Romanian television on 22 December 1989; see Cullen 1990)

Romania lies in south-eastern Europe. It is a large country (91,725 square miles) in comparison with its smaller neighbours. Romania has a population of 21.48 million.[1] The capital city is Bucharest, the language Romanian, and the currency is the Romanian Leu. The legal system is based upon the continental European model with a written constitution which was brought into force from 1991. The government is formed by the majority party (or parties)[2] with the Prime Minister chosen by the party (or parties) and nominated by the President (as the head of state) before the Parliament-elect. There is a semi-parliamentary system with two legislative bodies: a Senate (*Senat*) and a Chamber of Deputies (*Camera Deputatilor*). The President since 2004 has been Mr Traian Basescu who was re-elected to this position in December 2009.

How the state is governed has changed over time since the fall of communism in 1989. Initially, after 1989, parliamentary representatives were elected from lists proposed by all parties for both the legislative bodies: the Senate and the Chamber of Deputies. There was no actual difference between the two representative bodies other than the number of votes needed; hence, with the two bodies having the same functions, there was massive confusion over law adoption, endless mediations, and uncertainty for the public about who had political power (Stefan 2009). Reform took place in 2008 with the proportional representation system being replaced by a uni-nominal (first-past-the-post) one, where a Senator now needs to win in a constituency of 160,000 voters, and a member of the Chamber of Deputies in a constituency of 70,000 voters (Stefan 2009). There are 135 members in the Senate and 330 in the Chamber of Deputies, with forty-two districts, each containing seats for senators and deputies.

4.2.2   Current Romanian energy policy

Romania is a relatively new entrant into the nuclear energy family; however, it was a founding member in 1957 of the International Atomic Energy Agency (IAEA),[3] an autonomous body that reports to the United Nations. While countries in the Western and Eastern world developed nuclear technology for military purposes, Romania developed nuclear technology for the primary purpose of supplying energy to its electricity grid; though it has been suggested that 'a covert nuclear weapons development program was pursued under the Ceausescu regime' briefly before he was overthrown (Nuclear Information Project 2005). Romania was also part of the Non-Aligned

Movement,[4] and consequently it is significant that, in seeking its place between the West and East, it chose Canadian technology for its nuclear power programme. Before the collapse of the communist regime, Ceausescu[5] had developed an isolationist economic approach coupled with grandiose schemes of excess (Calinescu et al. 1991). This economic policy befell all types of infrastructure projects and the energy sector was no exception. While coal was the dominant fuel for electrical power, in keeping with the ambitions of Ceausescu, the development of nuclear technology was never far away. Ceausescu's regime had first considered nuclear technology in the 1960s, and support increased for this technology as a result of high losses in electrical transmission which resulted in frequent blackouts in the late 1970s and 1980s (Turnock 2007).

During the communist era, Romania's electricity was mainly consumed by industrial and commercial users (Wolak 2000). However, after the re-foundation of the Romanian state post-1989, electricity consumption dramatically decreased. This is evident in Table 4.2 and Romania has not yet returned to the same levels of usage pre-1989. However, as Table 4.3 demonstrates, Romania has ambitions to become an electricity exporter to other Central and Eastern European countries. So while consumption levels are expected to return to pre-1989 levels, it will be achieved through new generation in Romania rather than its previous reliance on imports from Russia.[6] The policy of decreasing dependence on Russia has continued, and the nuclear energy project continued post-1989, although with just one unit rather than five. Further, the possibility of entry to the EU which would inevitably lead to the decrease of thermal power production was another reason to continue with the nuclear project.

The 2008 electricity production mix can be seen in Table 4.3, with estimates included for 2015 and 2020. Whilst Romania owns a diverse but relatively limited amount of primary energy resources – such as oil, gas, lignite, uranium and renewable energy – these resources are for the most part being depleted (Prodea et al. 2008).

The Romanian electricity market restructured itself in compliance with the relevant European Union directives (Diaconu et al. 2009). It was horizontally separated into the following structure:

Table 4.2 Electricity Net Consumption in Romania

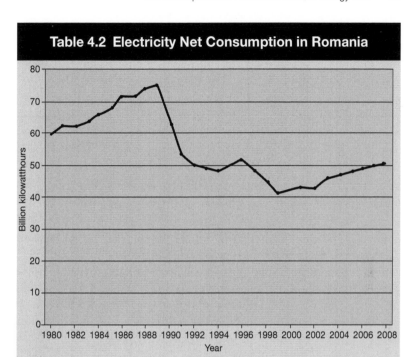

Source: US Energy Information Administration Statistics – Romania 2008

Table 4.3 Electricity production by source in Romania

Electricity production	2009	2015	2020
Domestic consumption (TWh)	64.2	74.5	85
Export (TWh)	3.5	15	15
Hydropower & renewable	28.8%	29%	32.5%
Nuclear	16%	24.1%	21.6%
Thermal – coal	39%	34.6%	34.9%
natural gas	14%	10.6%	9.5%
crude oil	2.2%	1.7%	1.5%

Source: Traicu 2008

(1) Hidroelectrica – operator of most of the country's hydroelectric capacity; (2) Termoelectrica – Romania's main thermal power generator; (3) Nuclearelectrica – operator of the country's nuclear capacity; (4) Transelectrica – the Transmission System Operator; (5) Electrica – operator of the country's distribution grid; and (6) OPCOM – the wholesale market operator. The distribution company has been further divided into eight regional companies, with four of these privatised and sold to foreign buyers (CEZ, E.ON, Electrica Banat, and Enel). In Romania, 17 per cent of the electricity generation market has been privatised, while 84 per cent of the market is open to consumers in terms of choosing a supplier (Pollitt 2009). Nuclearelectrica operates Romania's two operational nuclear reactors at Cernavoda, 50km from the Black Sea. Initial reports expect that the part-complete reactors Cernavoda 3 (17 per cent complete) and Cernavoda 4 (15 per cent complete) will be completed at some stage in the future; however, the fifth will not be completed.

4.2.3   Charting nuclear new build in Romania – Cernavoda

Phase 1 – the communist era, 1957–89
After the Second World War Romania became a communist state under the influence of the Soviet Union. Its first foray into nuclear activity began with the construction of the Soviet Nuclear Research Reactor VVR-S in 1957, which was built in the town of Magurele just outside the city limits of Bucharest.[7] In the early 1970s plans to develop a civil nuclear programme accelerated. Initial site investigations were carried out, with 100 potential sites located. The nuclear programme at that time was envisaged as involving the construction of ten reactors (units) over a fifteen-year period. A contract was signed with AECL in 1978 for the engineering and procurement for the first plant at Cernavoda. However, the plans for the nuclear energy programme were altered so that four reactors would be built at Cernavoda; subsequently in 1982, the government decided to include a fifth.

In spring 1979 the Ceausescu administration set forth a schedule of planning activities. This schedule initially involved the completion within eighty-five months of all five plants initially, which was then reduced to sixty months with a completion date set for 1985. Ongoing delays led to problems with the financial agreements which resulted in a break in the line of credit from the external investors in 1982. The net result was a huge delay to the schedule. In addition, the technicians were facing a myriad of inter-related problems. There was a constant fight to observe all the necessary safety conditions for a nuclear project, continuous pressure from the government to finish, contractors were making mistakes, and there were lots of non-conformities. This situation continued up until 1989 as the completion schedule for the project continued to be pushed ever forward.

Phase 2 – post-communism and Cernavoda 1: 1989–2010
Post-1989, and with the fall of communism, the situation changed. The first step was to develop a consortium with the owner (Romania), AECL and Ansaldo to finish the project. Work and finance stopped for the other four reactors, with the focus switched to Unit 1. The construction process began again in 1991, and Unit 1 was completed and came into operation in 1996. External assistance accelerated the project, while finance was received from the State budget, AECL and Ansaldo.

An investor agreement was signed in May 2001 to complete Cernavoda 2: it involved the same consortium and Unit 1 was used as financial collateral for Unit 2. Romania also took more of a role in this project, and was successful in seeking a €223.5 million loan from Euratom, and €218 million loan from Canada (Froggatt et al. 2007). Though the previous progress on the construction of Unit 2 had been minimal, construction began again in 2003 and it was finished in 2007. There were key differences in the planning of Unit 2 and these included: the ability to select suppliers from a world market; the experience of Unit 1; and an improved management structure which involved the same consortium as for Unit 1.

The conditions for building Units 3 and Unit 4 are different from the build processes of the previous two units. Units 3 and 4 are near replicas of the other already-built units and consequently the government is confident of a build process lasting sixty to sixty-eight months. Furthermore, Romania has become a member of the EU and different rules of investment apply, with corporate governance a factor and the advantage of sourcing investors from anywhere globally. Eventually six investors were chosen for the Cernavoda 3 and 4 project: Arcelor-Mittal, CEZ, Electrabel, Enel, Iberdrola and RWE. They were to own 49 per cent of the newly formed company Ergonuclear, which will own the two units. Nuclearelectrica (the government-owned nuclear company) will own the other 51 per cent of this company. This followed a previous Romanian government decision which had been to have only a 20 per cent stake for Nuclearelectrica with the investors providing the remaining 80 per cent of the financial capital.

The decision to revert to Nuclearlectrica holding 51 per cent was held to have its origin in the aim to increase energy security for Romania but there is perhaps also a political economy perspective, with the government not wanting to lose central control of the energy supply. Hence, Nuclearelectrica was to go into partnership with its six partners for Cernavoda, where two 706MW reactors (3 and 4) will be built. The contract, which was estimated by Romania to be worth €4 billion, involved Romania's investor partners having specific shares: GDF Suez (9.15 per cent), RWE (9.15 per cent), CEZ (9.15 per cent), Enel (9.15 per cent), Iberdrola (6.2 per cent) and ArcelorMittal (6.2 per cent). However, the percentage of ownership was then to decrease for Nuclearelectrica as Romania suffered heavily during the financial crisis of 2007–10, while Nuclearelectrica itself had to postpone its plans to go public on the Romanian stock exchange. The project, which Romania expected to take seventy-seven months to deliver, required final approval from the EC, and AECL was to supply the technology. In July 2010 Nuclearelectrica announced it would decrease its share to 20 per cent because of doubts regarding whether it had access to the funds to supply 51 per cent of the cost. Further, CEZ announced that it would withdraw from the project in September 2010. The other investment partners announced that they were willing to increase their shareholding but a new investment agreement was forecast for 2011. However, while the Romanian government were confident of the project not being delayed, questions remained as to whether some of the other investors would withdraw from the project also. In 2011 RWE and GDFSuez also withdrew from the project. China signed a preliminary agreement to take a stake in the next nuclear project in 2013 but this resulted in Enel and ArcelorMittal withdrawing.

Phase 3 – the 2020 project: 2020 and beyond
A new nuclear energy project is being planned in Romania for 2020. However, the criteria for choosing the technology are to be revised. Technical and economic performance will be instrumental but other key factors will be the site, finance, local contribution and undoubtedly politics, while the competition and state aid rules of the EU community will have to be followed. The analysis aims to show the better technology choice though this will need government support. However, the government in Romania has been changing too often for any concrete decision to be made just yet. However, Romania is familiar with CANDU technology so there would be benefits from choosing this technology once again.

The advantage of the CANDU-6 reactor technology has been Romania's ability to control the nuclear fuel cycle. Since it has the infrastructure still in place, this could provide future cost savings in a nuclear project through having the nuclear fuel as well as the expertise. The two reactors in operation at Cernavoda are CANDU-6 natural uranium fuelled heavy water cooled and moderated reactors. A CANDU-6 nuclear power system does not require enriched fuel and so enrichment activities do not form part of the Romanian nuclear fuel cycle. Romania has several uranium mines and produces its own sinterable UO2 powder and sintered UO2 fuel pellets. Furthermore, Romania already has a facility that produces the qualified CANDU-6 fuel for use in the nuclear energy reactors at Cernavoda. Importantly, however, and as part of Ceauşescu's vision of self-reliance, Romania also developed perhaps the most technologically demanding aspect of a CANDU-6 fuel cycle: the production of heavy water for reactor moderation and cooling (Nuttall 2010). Just a small amount of heavy water is needed for each nuclear reactor and most of the heavy water needed has been produced for plants Cernavoda 3 and 4. This is an advantage for investors in Cernavoda 3 and 4, and the facilities could also be used in a different project.

Nevertheless, Romania, because of its EU member state status, has to consider supporting EU products. Hence, the modern pressurised water reactor (PWR) from France is a contender, so in this context the developments in Finland and France where PWRs are currently being built will be followed.

There are other hurdles that Romania has to resolve too. The general level of educational qualifications is quite low and the education system quite isolated. There need to be more specialist schools to increase high-level qualifications, more programmes of cooperation with other countries, and an educational programme designed to encourage the young to specialise in nuclear energy. These factors may be highlighted further by the financial crisis (2007–2010) that engulfed Romania. Overall, the Romanian stock exchange composite index BET-C fell over 50 per cent during the crisis. Romania was promised significant investment from external organisations since 2009, including the International Monetary Fund (IMF, €12.95 billion), the EU (€5 billion), the World Bank (€1 billion), and the European Bank for Reconstruction and Development (EBRD, €1 billion). Indeed, some institutions forecast that the Romanian economy would collapse in 2011 (ECIR 2010). The economic crisis will definitely delay the start of 2020 project, and while investor support remains strong for the Cernavoda Unit 3 and 4 project, it has yet to be fully finalised.

4.3   Focusing on Romanian energy law and policy: hypotheses analyses

4.3.1   Hypothesis 1: The law in the electricity sector is weak and insufficient in Romania

Academic literature cites the weakness of the legal structures in the electricity sector both pre- and post-1989 (Wolak 2000; Diaconu et al. 2009; Jora 2006). Indeed, a report prepared for the UN[8] highlighted the significant legal reforms and challenges that Romania faced prior to its accession into the EU in 2007. Further, it is also acknowledged by other authors that Romania is still lacking in the development of law in many areas (Gallagher 2009). However, despite this, the research conducted in the interviews opposes this view, in particular in the case of the nuclear energy sector in Romania. Therefore the hypothesis has been unproven, and while legislation may be deficient in other areas of the economy, in the electricity sector and in particular the nuclear energy sector, legislation is strong and so too its application. In the analysis that follows and for the rest of this section, specific quotes or opinions gathered from the interview process are referenced with an interview code that corresponds to those listed in the Appendix, with a letter and number corresponding to the institution of the interviewee.

The nuclear energy sector was characterised by a lack of legislation before the fall of communism (I-6). Prior to 1989 legal and democratic structures in many sectors did not exist and if they did, they were subject to constant change. Following the 1989 revolution this scenario continued in other sectors of the economy, though not in the energy sector (I-5, I-6, I-10). However, the nuclear sector was forced to change in a legal context in particular in relation to its safety regulations. Romania was under immense pressure from the IAEA and AECL in this regard (I-6, I-10). Consequently, the National Commission for the Control of Nuclear Activities (CNCAN)[9] was established in 1990. To accelerate its ability to apply the law, the personnel assigned to this body were trained extensively by the Canadian regulatory equivalent (AECB)[10] for four years and links still exist between both bodies (I-5, I-10). CNCAN is the most important organisation from a legal standpoint in the nuclear energy sector in Romania. It is the regulatory body responsible for the safety of all nuclear activities in Romania and is under the coordination of the Prime Minister, and not just the Ministry for Commerce, which presides over the other energy sources. Its main duties cover safety issues relating to the siting, construction, operation and decommissioning of nuclear installations in Romania.[11]

It was not until 1996 that key legislation on nuclear energy was enacted into Romanian law despite the country's first reactor going into operation in the same year – Law No. 111/1996, which was first published on 29 October 1996.[12] The object of the law is the safe conduct of nuclear activities for exclusively peaceful purposes so that they meet safety conditions set out for the protection of professionally exposed personnel, the general population, the environment and property. The law aims to minimise the risks associated with nuclear activities through a regime of regulatory requirements and compliance with international conventions. It provides the legal framework for the regulation, licensing, control of operational activities, and safety and waste management issues involving the peaceful uses of nuclear energy.

Romania does recognise, however, the need for further change in the nuclear legal sector. This is in particular so that the second phase of nuclear power can be delivered in a much smoother process (I-5, 6). Three key areas of reform have emerged:

1. CNCAN needs to be reformed with personnel being a key issue (I-7). For the continued development and successful operation of the nuclear sector, it must have good employees to ensure both public and investor confidence (I-5, I-6, I-10). Salaries for personnel need to be increased so as to attract the top personnel in the sector to this agency; furthermore, this could be funded by the licensing fees.

2. Planning law needs to be more open, transparent and clear, so that planning practice is clearly established, not just for the current two units being planned but also for the 2020 nuclear project.

3. The legal responsibilities of the utility company (Nuclearelectrica) need to be increased (I-5, I-6). This company should have a clear responsibility for educating government members, other politicians and the public on the sector. It should also develop proper decision-making processes that can be tracked so as to ensure safety, timeliness, budgetary and good project management throughout the build phase of the nuclear project.

These changes will further enhance investor and public belief in nuclear energy and ensure that the nuclear energy law in Romania is seen as proactive rather than reactive.

However, there are emerging legal issues that need to be resolved too. These emanate from the plan to build reactors 3 and 4 on the Cernavoda site. These include the operation and maintenance of the plant and site – which will be owned by two separate companies, Nuclearelectrica and Ergonuclear – as well as the provision of nuclear fuel and the question of liability. The problem arises as to the transfer of resources between these latter two companies, and whether this transfer would constitute a form of State aid to the Cernavoda 3 and 4 project. Concerning the liability issue, if there is an accident on site and the reactors need to be shut down, the question arises as to which company will be liable. These concerns will need to be expressly detailed in the final investor agreement for Cernavoda 3 and 4, and for the new nuclear project in 2020.

4.3.2 Hypothesis 2: EU entry was not significant for the nuclear sector in terms of legal development

This was because interviewees believed that nuclear law had been applied prior to EU entry and in 1996 when the first reactor went into operation at Cernavoda 1. Academic authors pointed towards Romania being slow to introduce EU law and not ensuring its full application in practice. Furthermore, these academic authors and interviewees held that the EU accession process had not resulted in significant legal and democratic development. However, some interviewees disagreed and held that EU membership had resulted in many legal benefits for the nuclear energy sector in Romania. This is evident through Romania adopting the Euratom Treaty, becoming part of research networks, work-exchange schemes, and availing itself of other EU expertise. It also meant that AECL had an operational reactor in Europe; having a good relationship with Romania would not only benefit AECL in terms of new business but also benefit Romania in terms of having a partner that would ensure operational safety. For these reasons that emanated from the interview analysis, the hypothesis was unproven.

Romania's entry to the EU demonstrated its full transition from communist state to EU Member State. Romania and Bulgaria joined the EU in 2007 in the fifth enlargement process of 2004–7. Notably, neither country was ready to join in 2004 when the other ten new countries joined. Romania adopted a significant proportion of EU law pre-accession in 2007.

A positive result of EU entry for Romania was enacting the transfer of the legislative aims of the Euratom Treaty into Romanian law (I-6). Romania has had a relatively painless process in terms of developing and applying law in the nuclear sector, since it has been guided by the EU and IAEA, both of which have provided funding for this purpose. The influence of AECL also needs to be noted as it does not have any other reactors in Europe. In the 1970s despite little legislation in the area, Ansaldo and AECL became involved in the first phase of the nuclear new build at Cernavoda. This raises the issue of how important national legislation is to a nuclear project. Nevertheless, with the continued development and improvement of the nuclear legal sector, more investors have been attracted to Romania who see an increasingly stable economy with clear legislation in the area, and notably interviewees stated even if it was for the requirements of the investors only (I-6, I-7, I-11, I-12).

The state-centrist nature of the Euratom Treaty offered benefits to Romania, as an emerging nuclear energy state (I-5, I-9). The Euratom Treaty permits a country to own its nuclear energy assets, and also holds that the EU will not play a role in or interfere with a country's nuclear energy policy. The IAEA supports Euratom in this regard, stating that 'each State must develop its own legislative framework based on its own situation, including its constitutional and legal framework, cultural traditions, scientific, technical and industrial capacities, and financial and human resources' (IAEA 2002). This allows an emerging nuclear energy state to develop and control its own nuclear energy sector and have energy policy flexibility (I-9). The significance of this is that while Romania has to comply with EU legislation on oil, gas, coal and renewables – where through the EU accession agreement it was obliged to shut down coal plants – the Euratom Treaty permits a country to control its own nuclear energy policy without interference (I-6, I-9). Further, agreements with external suppliers of technology and investors may be more flexible than in a more developed economy (I-6).

Euratom legislation on competition and State aid for the nuclear energy sector is different. It is different from the same legislation applicable to all other industries in the EU internal market. These different rules make it an attractive sector for investors (I-11, I-12). This is witnessed where the state company in charge of nuclear energy (Nuclearelectrica) has assumed the insurance responsibility for the nuclear sector (I-6, I-12), though this is not specific to just Romania. There are further examples of State aid in the nuclear sector in Romania.[13] In comparison with the first phase of nuclear new build, in the second phase many of the legal issues surrounding State aid and competition are expected to be resolved (I-6).

Romania under the guidance of the EU has updated its existing regulatory and licensing framework, one that has the five required central tenets sought by investors: predictability, stability, timeliness, national coordination and international alignment (European Nuclear Energy Forum 2008). This was not the case for the first phase, and the evidence is that Romania is availing itself of EU expertise to improve its nuclear energy sector. It is also taking advantage of research networks and work-exchange schemes (I-6, I-11, I-12). Romania is still in a formative stage of its nuclear energy programme, and EU investors and EU technology providers can influence change which is an attraction for these companies (I-6, I-11, I-12). Further, EU membership has provided an opportunity to build a relationship with France, on whose nuclear energy strategy Romania has modelled its own. Romania views nuclear energy as playing a leading role in its energy strategy, with an increase from 16 per cent to 40 per cent or even 60 per cent electricity share envisaged by 2020 (I-5). These latter actions that emanate from its EU membership have further aided Romania's ability to attract investors to supply the finance for nuclear new build (I-11, I-12, I-13).

4.3.3   Hypothesis 3: The IAEA has played an important role in the Romanian nuclear energy programme

The literature argues that the IAEA has been of importance to the development of nuclear energy programmes in many countries and Romania is no exception. Many of the interviewees for this research agreed with this hypothesis. However, this interviewee agreement with the hypothesis was limited and consequently the hypothesis was unproven. The IAEA played a role in ensuring the continuation of the build process for Cernavoda 1 post the fall of communism, and it conducted a full inspection of all Romanian facilities. However, apart from that involvement, the IAEA has played a limited role in Romania and continues to do so. This is demonstrated by the fact that Romania did not adhere to the IAEA protocol for building a nuclear power plant.

Romania has skipped IAEA legal steps in its nuclear build process. However, despite this, it has operational and safe nuclear reactors. If one examines the IAEA milestones for nuclear new build – as demonstrated in Table 4.4 – it seems that Romania has in the past skipped numerous processes and has sought tenders and engaged in construction contracts prior to doing several other pieces of

Table 4.4 IAEA milestones for nuclear new build

Milestone	Project process	Timeline
Milestone 1: Ready to make a knowledgeable commitment to a nuclear power programme	Consideration before a decision to proceed with a nuclear power programme is taken	Pre-project
	Preparatory work for NPP construction	Project decision-making
Milestone 2: Ready to invite bids for first nuclear power plant (NPP)	Legislative framework Regulatory framework Human resources Preliminary siting Funding & financing	
	Activities to implement NPP Tendering	
	Construction contract	Construction
Milestone 3: Ready to commission and operate first NPP	Site licence Design approval Construction licence Electricity grid	
	Security & physical protection	Operation
	Radioactive waste Operation licence	(10–15 year process)

Source: Adapted by the author from IAEA (2007)

preparatory work for nuclear new build, such as having a definitive legislative framework; regulatory framework; human resources; and funding and financing. The first reactor was built and in operation by 1996, the same year that nuclear law came into existence. Human resources, funding and financing were all issues in the first phase of nuclear new build and this resulted in delays to the project.

Nevertheless, the Romanian case demonstrates the importance and unimportance of the IAEA milestones. Proceeding in accordance with these milestones might have reduced the delays in the first phase of the Romanian nuclear project, which still remains unfinished. On the other hand, it demonstrates that steps can be skipped even if a country intends to develop nuclear energy, and it will not hinder the completion of some or all of the project (I-5, I-6). Hence, there are important lessons from the Romanian project that can be incorporated into other nuclear energy projects under consideration in other countries. Further, three other countries – UAE, Jordan and Vietnam – have been identified that are running, or have conducted, tendering and construction contract negotiations without the necessary nuclear legislative framework being in place (IAEA 2007).

The Romanian case highlights how a country can fast-track a nuclear new build process (I-5, I-12). There were many other factors that led to delay in the Romanian nuclear project – as will be outlined later – and not all the blame for the delays can be attributed to Romania not following the IAEA milestones for nuclear new build. The Romanian project does signal a shift to focusing on procurement first for nuclear projects, and then switching the focus to legislative and regulatory frameworks where safety in design, construction and operation of the nuclear reactor are paramount (I-6, I-9, I-12, I-13). Further, the Romanian case highlights that this focus on procurement has an advantage in that it, in essence, sub-contracts the legal framework to the external partners chosen after the procurement process. In this regard, the Romanian nuclear energy project has benefited from its external partner AECL, which as mentioned earlier, assisted in the project and continues to do so in a major way.

The question therefore arises as to how important is the successful operation of nuclear law in a country or indeed the influence of the IAEA? In Romania, the investors were willing and did enter into contracts to construct and supply the nuclear energy project at Cernavoda despite knowledge of poor legal structures in the nuclear sector and other sectors of the economy. Further, these same investors were knowledgeable about the many other legal issues that emerged in Romania regarding nuclear energy: a personnel shortage; issues of legal enforcement; attempts by Romania to dominate contract negotiations; State company reform/privatisation; and State aid and competition concerns (I-5, I-6, I-7, I-12, I-13). Investors were willing to enter for strategic reasons, so as to have a presence in

Central and Eastern, and to use the Romanian project to achieve that goal and gain more customers. The lack of strength and application of legal structures in the nuclear energy sector and other economic sectors did not pose a problem. Investors were willing to take over the role of providing safety and ensuring with the national regulators that the highest safety measures were employed (I-5, I-8, I-9). While there was knowledge that the legal structures would improve, Romania highlights the importance of having an active investor in the project which has other reasons to ensure safety and train the local population to a good standard. For developing countries that intend to begin a nuclear power programme, this will be a significant consideration in their nuclear new build plans.

4.3.4   Hypothesis 4: Ceausescu had a destructive influence on the development of the Romanian energy sector

Interviewees and the academic literature both state the destructive influence of Ceausescu on the Romanian energy sector and in particular the nuclear energy sector. However, other interviewees disagreed in relation to the nuclear energy sector. The hypothesis was unproven as the evidence points towards Ceausescu having had a more positive than negative influence on the nuclear energy sector. This is because Romanian energy policy was not unique to Ceausescu. It was always dominated by politics, both pre- and post- the Ceausescu regime. Although under Ceausescu, no reactor was fully completed nor went into operation, he did influence energy policy after the fall of communism. Since 1990 energy policy has been at the core of policy considerations in successive Romanian governments. Two nuclear reactors were completed with the aim of reducing the Romania's energy dependence on Russia. The independence he sought for the sector in forcing it to produce a percentage of components for each reactor has left Romania with its own small nuclear energy industry. Of more significance was that Ceausescu had a long-term vision for the nuclear energy sector, and this thinking has been retained by the Romanian government which is one of the few EU governments to have a long-term energy policy.

Energy policy in Romania has always been dominated by politics. During the Second World War, Romania, as an ally of Germany, provided the latter with equipment and much of its own oil (Craciunoiu et al. 1995). Under Ceausescu the Romanian government played a more than dominant role in the development of the energy sector, in particular by developing its nuclear energy sector. In the first phase, Canada's AECL was chosen as the technology provider. This appealed to Ceausescu who – despite leading a communist state – wanted to gain favour in Western world (I-1, I-10). A technology provider has not yet been chosen for the new 2020 project (four reactors at a new site in Romania where construction is planned to begin in 2020). However, it seems that again the decision will be made by government and it will be a contentious matter both nationally and internationally. The choice that rests with Romania is whether to choose Canadian or French technology. Romania has concerns in this regard in particular because of its EU status (I-10). As an EU Member State, it feels obligated to follow and support EU products and technology and thus Areva from France has become the preferred choice of the government (I-4, I-5, I-6, I-10).

The leading role played by the government in Romania in the nuclear energy sector produced negative results prior to the emergence of democracy (after the fall of communism) in 1989. Ceausescu's visions were excessive for the sector and they slowed down the development of the sector to a substantial degree (I-1, I-2, I-11). Ceausescu had even appointed some of his party colleagues, who were uneducated and unfamiliar with the sector, to management roles in the project. Many of the delays can be traced to the meddling influence of Ceausescu. With Ceausescu in power, decision-making in the nuclear energy sector was concentrated within the confines of his own office or those people in close proximity to the dictator (I-1, I-2). For example, as the project progressed, Ceausescu placed many of his allies into various management positions in the project (I-1, I-2). Their lack of expertise in the area contributed to further delays as operations gradually became slower and slower. The effect of actions such as these was to cause delays to the project which is evident in the construction process – despite the process beginning in 1979, the first reactor was not completed until 1996, seventeen years later. However, long construction times are not unique to Romania, and occur in many other countries too.

A further Romanian policy was to promote energy security. In this regard Ceausescu was very ambitious, for he had a long-term vision to ensure Romanian energy independence (I-1, I-2, I-5). Initially, in the planning phase that began circa 1970–1 and lasted until 1979, Ceausescu had visions of building ten reactors and then subsequently eight reactors, with four at two sites. Finally a plan was agreed upon that involved the construction of four reactors at Cernavoda, all to be built within eighty-five months, later reduced to sixty months with a fifth plant added to the plan in 1982. At one time there were 15,000 people working side by side on the five reactors (I-2, I-3, I-5). While this policy of energy security is one that is promoted at the moment in Romania and by the EU itself, Romania may have benefited from a gradual development of energy security. A lesson can be identified in the Romania case that when aiming to achieve too quickly an increase in energy security, delay may be a major factor in many projects.

Romania also tried to seek independence in its nuclear programme. This involved each Ministry being involved in the production of new components for the four reactors (I-1, I-2). Huge technical programmes were started. Over the course of the project, 50 per cent of the components were to be manufactured within Romania for Unit 1, with this increasing to 90 per cent for Units 3 and 4 (I-1, I-5). This policy resulted in decreased work on site, delays and the build schedules being extended. Despite these negatives, the provision of 50 per cent of components coming from Romania itself was nearly achieved for Unit 1 (I-1, I-2). Nevertheless, this contributed to a significant portion of the delays, as there was a severe lack of expertise in the sector. The policy failed for the most part and demonstrates why a possible new entrant to the nuclear new build industry should not set out to achieve this aim. However, it has created a small but vibrant nuclear industry for components and expertise in Romania itself.

The role of the democratic government of Romania has improved over the last two decades. It has accelerated the completion times for the nuclear project in comparison with the previous communist government. In this regard, under its management, Unit 1 took six years to complete (having been 35 per cent completed in terms of construction), while Unit 2 (30 per cent completed) took just four years. The post-communist government has shown as strong a commitment to nuclear as Ceausescu and, in particular, this is evident in that four-year build process for the Cernavoda Unit 2 project when it was re-started (I-5). It is also noticeable that, with the 2020 project, preparations have begun already well in advance. Nuclear energy now plays a predominant role in the energy sector[14] – evidenced by the government's commitment to the 2020 project (I-6). This determination and demonstration of long-term commitment attracts investors who know that government support and a long-term energy strategy with a focus on nuclear power reduce the risk of their investment (I-5, I-12). Further, Romania aims to have between 40 and 60 per cent of its electricity provided by nuclear power, and harbours the hope of being like France in terms of its large nuclear capacity and ability to export power (I-5, I-10). Nevertheless, questions have being raised over the government appointees to investor negotiations on the project who have attempted to influence proceedings in a negative fashion (I-12, I-13).

The Romanian nuclear industry has also benefited from other policy mechanisms. The economy has benefited from the government policy of continued incentives for Romanian firms which continue in, or wish to enter, the supply chain for the nuclear sector (I-6). The development of the Romanian economy itself can be seen in its entry into the EU (2007). The EU accession agreement for Romania required the closure of Romania's thermal power plants, and this has put nuclear energy and its continued development at the forefront of its energy policy (I-8, I-9). Associated with this is the continued strategy of decreasing its dependency upon natural gas, which in effect is a strategy to increase nuclear, so as to decrease its dependency upon Russia; in this way one of Ceausescu's policies survives (I-1, I-2).

4.3.5 Hypothesis 5: There is widespread dissemination of information on the Romanian nuclear energy sector

This hypothesis is supported by the literature and interviewees. However, many interviewees oppose this assertion, and the research conducted supports the opposing view. Therefore the hypothesis is unproven. This is because information and knowledge on the nuclear energy sector remains with an elite in Romania. The majority of the population are unaware of the energy sector and while public participation in public consultations on nuclear energy is increasing, it is because it has started from such a low base. Further, there is no opposition to nuclear energy, so there is a concern regarding the independence of the information. The Romanian government has not given sufficient financial resources to independent firms to educate the public nor has it provided educational institutions with sufficient financial resources to attract students to study nuclear energy. Instead Romania relies upon its external partners to the nuclear project to make up the shortfalls in knowledge. Consequently, there is no widespread dissemination of information on the sector and it remains with an elite group supported by the external partners.

Information exchange in the nuclear energy sector has been poor since the emergence of the sector in Romania. Top-down decision-making has been widespread in the sector and has contributed to the lack of information dissemination within the sector. Knowledge of the sector has remained within an elite group of Romanian society and this remains the case as Romania sets out on a second phase of nuclear new build (I-8, I-10). Not only are safety and legal organisations in the sector underfunded, but the education system for the next generation in nuclear is also in need of reform (I-8, I-10). The combination of these factors means that public participation in nuclear projects is very low and though improving is doing so from a very low base. It is a problem in need of urgent action.

The diversity of views that emanate from the nuclear energy sector demonstrates the key problem areas for the future of the sector in Romania. There are major discrepancies between the opinions of nuclear sector workers, government action and national reports for the sector:

1. The first of these is the example of the supply of expertise in the nuclear field. Leading Romanian academics predict a shortfall in the engineering and physics students who specialise in nuclear energy (Petra et al. 2008; Constantin and Hristea 2008). The

numbers of students going to study in this area are falling and calls for the government to increase funding in education have not yet met a response; this despite the government announcing plans for a further nuclear power project containing four reactors and the ambition to develop a similar capability to France. Furthermore, educational re-organisation, which could potentially have a positive response on student numbers, is needed (Ghiordanescu et al. 2008). Romanian academics criticise the EU Bologna educational system which has reduced university education to three years, in that it does not allow sufficient time for profound assimilation of basic knowledge in nuclear energy and physics (I-8, I-9, I-10).

2. A second example concerns the supply of uranium in Romania, a debated issue among government, industry and academic circles. Sources suggest that Romanian supplies will last until roughly between 2015 and 2020 (Traicu 2009). No account, however, appears to have been taken of possible increases in prices to long-term operational cost structures, even though there is international debate as to whether uranium will make a significant impact on cost structure (Forsberg 2010; Massachusetts Institute of Technology 2010).

4.3.6   Hypothesis 6: The energy sector and politicians have too strong a relationship in Romania

Politics is considered by many academic authors and interviewees to be too influential in Romanian policy development and in particular in the energy sector. However, there is an opposing view that the government needs to remain heavily involved in the energy sector for specific and important reasons for Romania. There was a range of contrasting viewpoints in the literature and the interviewees, and therefore this was investigated and the hypothesis was proven. However, the interview evidence demonstrates that a strong government involvement in the energy sector can be advantageous. Of most importance is that a government recognise that the energy sector should operate in and for the long-term. Hence, government support in terms of decision-making and providing financial resources should be part of a continuous government policy. Romanian politicians have recognised this, and there is cross-party support for the continued progress of the nuclear energy sector and the central role that nuclear energy has in its energy policy. Political support for nuclear energy policy has always been strong. Notably, Romanian politicians across all parties are in favour of a long-term energy policy with nuclear energy at its core. This has increased the willingness of investors to consider investing in Cernavoda 3 and 4 – with up to thirty initial applications before this was narrowed down to six (I-6, I-11, I-12, I-13). Despite the financial crisis that began in 2007, these investors remained on board despite a small number eventually opting out (I-6).

There is a realisation in Romania that energy and energy projects have a long-term nature. The political decision-making and economic policy action at the highest political level reflect this; Romania has long-term plans to develop further nuclear power plants such as the 2020 project and aims to have the ability to export electricity. Further, the Romanian government continues to demonstrate a keen willingness to invest in nuclear projects themselves (I-5, I-7). However, these political decisions and aims are not supported by actual investment in the entire nuclear value chain (I-10). As stated previously, action to engage with the education of the public on nuclear and to educate future nuclear sector personnel has been limited – both of which will inhibit the long-term energy policy goals of Romania.

The external influence of project partners and other countries has been significant in Romania, and has contributed to the success of nuclear energy there (I-5). As stated previously, the Romanian government has been influenced by its ambitions to be a nuclear energy power like France, and by its entry into the EU. However, Russia has also played a defining role (I-1, I-2). Romania's mistrust of Russia, which once had aims to make Romania into an 'agriculture state', continues. Romania's efforts to decrease its energy dependence on Russia are part of the reason for first entering into the nuclear family, and this mission still continues today. Canada and its nuclear company AECL and Italy's ANSALDO have also played a significant role in assisting the first phase of nuclear new build in Romania. They have been involved since the 1970s, and have remained involved despite the effects of Ceausescu's interference, the subsequent fall of communism and the chaos of the transition to democracy. This demonstrates the power of the commitment to a corporate strategy in energy firms in relation to the nuclear energy sector, and provides a lesson for emerging nuclear states.

4.4 Conclusion

This chapter assesses why Romania was successful in developing a civil nuclear power programme despite political, economic and social turbulence. It reveals that Romania progressed in its plans to build nuclear despite political turmoil associated with the transition from communism to democracy. However, Romania has a comparatively different political history to its Central and Eastern European neighbours in that from the 1960s onwards it developed a serious mistrust of Russia. This is demonstrated in its choice of the Canadian AECL CANDU reactor as its nuclear technology, which is the only time AECL has sold its technology in Europe. Development of the nuclear energy sector was instrumental in decreasing Romania's dependency on Russia, and this policy is still active.

The diversity of views that emanate from the nuclear energy sector in Romania highlights a key problem area for the future of the sector in Romania. The nuclear sector has always been led by an elite who have the knowledge and do not distribute it, a situation largely unchanged since the Ceausescu era. Indeed, the lack of social, legal and political change post-1989 contributed to the continuation of top-down policy decisions and there still exists little information exchange, public debate or public participation. University education and consequently public participation processes in the nuclear sector are underfunded despite the government rhetoric of its ambitious plans for nuclear energy in the future.

Romania has, however, developed the beginning of a nuclear power programme successfully despite the lengthy times it has taken to bring the reactors into operation. There are two nuclear reactors in operation at Cernavoda – in operation since 1996 and 2007 – with a further two in a very advanced planning stage and a separate new project which is planned to be completed by 2020. As a member of the EU, Romania feels obliged to choose France's Areva EPR technology; however, the infrastructure exists already in Romania for the Canadian CANDU technology.

Romania's entry to the EU completed the full transition of Romania from communist state to EU Member State and it has had a positive effect. EU entry necessitated enacting the transfer of the legislative aims of the Euratom Treaty and IAEA regulations into Romanian law. However, Romania has skipped IAEA legal steps in its nuclear build process and consequently the Romanian case highlights how a country can fast-track a nuclear new build process. Ambitious energy policy can deliver.

The question does arise however: how important is the successful operation of international nuclear law and a legal system in a potential civilian nuclear country? The answer is, it is not that important, although safety in nuclear operations is a global concern. From a Romanian perspective, its nuclear energy sector was characterised by a lack of legislation before the fall of communism in 1989. It was not until 1996 that key legislation on nuclear energy was enacted into Romanian law, the same year the first reactor came into operation. Further, the legal system was in a constant state of revision until Romania joined the EU, and Romania's entry (along with that of Bulgaria) to the EU was delayed from 2004 to 2007. The view exists from some scholars that it was still not ready in 2007, and this apprehension was later expressed by the EU.

Romania does, however, recognise the need for further changes to the legal system and the nuclear legal sector, and is proactive in that regard. These changes aim to enhance investor and public belief in nuclear energy and ensure that the nuclear energy policy of Romania is seen as proactive rather than reactive. There are other positives too in that there is a realisation in Romania that energy and energy projects have a long-term nature. This is represented by the shared common agreement among all political parties on the direction of Romanian energy policy despite many differences in other policy areas. There is political willingness to move along nuclear projects. Further, the Romanian government has always understood the role of its external partners in the nuclear project and their contribution to the success of the project. In effect, the safety regime for the nuclear power project is outsourced to the external partner(s). Hence, international nuclear legal obligations are addressed but essentially, at first, through the external partner, and subsequently through cooperative learning programmes with the external partner and international agencies.

Romania is an example to other emerging civilian nuclear nations. Despite political, legal and social turbulence, and consequently poor structures and institutions in place in all those spheres, it has successfully developed a nuclear power programme. Of significance is that legal and institutional development has not been a hindrance to nuclear energy development. Further, external actors can play a key role in 'legitimising' the project. As the Romanian case demonstrates, there need not be undue concern over the ability of developing nations and even developed nations to begin a civil nuclear power programme.

Energy Law and Policy Development in the US Nuclear Energy Industry: A Three State Analysis

5.1 Introduction

This chapter examines nuclear energy policy across three states in the United States – Georgia, Pennsylvania and Texas – during 1990–2010. Therefore, the nuclear energy crisis at Fukushima in Japan March 2011 is beyond the scope of this research. Nevertheless, the fundamental conclusions of this research remain valid, as the impact of Fukushima is not yet fully known and in addition the US has experienced its own crisis at Three Mile Island, which has shaped its own nuclear industry to an extent already.

The chapter provides a unique example of energy law and policy development through insights gained through a unique comparison of US states that have deregulated, regulated and 'hybrid' electricity markets. It is evident that law can play an effective central role in the development of the nuclear energy sector, and the role of state-driven policy in the nuclear energy sector is fundamental to delivering on policy.

5.2 Choosing three US states: Pennsylvania, Texas and Georgia

The decision to choose these three states was based on their characteristics, which demonstrated their value as a representative sample of states within the US: Pennsylvania is a member of PJM (a liberalised electricity market formed of thirteen states and the District of Columbia; the name PJM reflects the first three member states: Pennsylvania, New Jersey and Maryland), and also the state where the 1979 Three Mile Island accident occurred; Texas is a 'hybrid' state in terms of having both regulated and deregulated electricity areas and, uniquely in the contiguous US, it has its own transmission system; and, finally, Georgia is a regulated state and also has the most advanced plans for nuclear new build in the US. Table 5.1 shows some basic features of the electricity and nuclear energy sectors within the three states. Knowledge of this information will be useful

Table 5.1 Electricity and nuclear statistics in Georgia, Pennsylvania and Texas in the US

Feature/State	Georgia	Pennsylvania	Texas
Population	9.68m	12.6m	24.8m
Electricity sector policy	Regulated	Deregulated (PJM)	Hybrid (ERCOT)
% share of nuclear energy in the electricity sector	23%	34%	10%
% share of coal, gas, renewables in the electricity sector	63% 10% 2%	54% 8% 3%	36% 49% 5%
Nuclear power plants	4	9	4
Planned nuclear power plants	2	1	6*
Companies Technology provider	1: Southern Nuclear 2: Types: General Electric, Westinghouse	4: First Energy, Entergy, PPL, Exelon 3: Westinghouse, General Electric, Babcock and Wilcox	2: Luminant Generation, STP Nuclear Westinghouse

*A more realistic number is two, however: plans were submitted by Exelon and Luminant Generation for two each, but these plans have since been suspended.

Source: Compiled by the author as of December 2010 from the US Energy Information Administration (2010) and US Nuclear Regulatory Commission (2010)

for the subsequent sections. The particular significance of Table 5.1 is that it shows that in late 2010 all three states had plans to build further nuclear power capacity.

The analysis that follows is based in part on the responses of those interviewed for the research. In the text analysis that follows, GI refers to a Georgian interview, and GI-1 identifies the inteviewee from the tables in the Appendix – the same applies for PI and TI, which refer to Pennsylvania and Texas interviews respectively. Further, some statements are supported by the majority view of critics or proponents of the hypothesis, and in these cases the reference code is either CVP (Consensus View of the Proponents), or CVC (Consensus View of the Critics).

5.3   Energy law and policy development in the nuclear energy sector in the US: uncontested issues

Nuclear energy in the US has significant competition as an electricity supply source, not just from coal and gas, but increasingly from renewable energy (wind in particular). Indeed, there is too much competition from other energy sources to enable nuclear energy expansion in some states in the US at present. Further, the potential of shale gas (for example, in Pennsylvania with the discovery of the Marcellus Shale gas reserves) is adding to the competition. Nevertheless, some interviewees expressed the view that nuclear energy is still needed; for example, one interviewee (TI-6) from Texas stated in this regard that:

> When you look at long term growth numbers, if the nuclear plants are not built, you are going to have to do a lot of something else, and I do not know who is ready to step up to that one yet, so from that point of view regulators and ERCOT people are keeping their fingers crossed, along with political figures, that the (nuclear) power plants will go ahead as otherwise we will have to do a lot of something else . . .

There are other factors that have played a role in nuclear energy development in the US, in particular, the regulator, the Nuclear Regulatory Commission (NRC). The NRC has struggled in the past in taking a long time to approve projects, and although it has undergone changes, there remains a need to improve:

> What impressed me about the NRC was their ability to make good technical decisions and that they made decisions. I was concerned before I went there. The fact that, you know, we had all heard that there had not been a new reactor license application since Three Mile Island. There were a lot of licenses in process but there had not been a new one. So I was concerned about the NRC's ability to make decisions but it turned out that that was an unfounded concern because they had done power upgrades, they had done license renewals so I was impressed with the agency. I thought they were a good focused organisation but like any organisation you can do much better. (GI-4)

Electricity policy suffers from fragmentation in the US, with each state having significant control of its own electricity policy – except for those in regional electricity markets, for example PJM. This fragmentation led to individual technical designs and, when coupled with the slow regulatory regime, contributed to slow construction times in the past. Further, the fragmentation resulted in the weakness of the financial capacity of energy companies in the US to build a new nuclear project, with companies operating within states and not having (without major public funds) access to the financial resources needed to build a nuclear power project.

Nuclear energy lobby groups are weak in comparison to environmental lobbying groups. For many years during the 1960s, nuclear had no need for lobbying because of the link between nuclear energy, the military and politics. As a result lobby groups, lobby formations and networks do not as readily exist or are at an earlier stage of development than lobby groups, networks and associations for other energy sources. A positive issue related to this is that environmental lobbying groups no longer see nuclear energy as the primary opposition. This is because of the association of nuclear energy with clean energy sources, in that it produces no carbon dioxide. Indeed, many environmental lobby groups are transferring their efforts to tackle carbon dioxide-producing energy sources.

Information dissemination about nuclear energy is not sufficient in the US. This is linked intrinsically to the problem of education on and surrounding nuclear energy issues. Nuclear energy is a complex subject and topic – there is an educational gap surrounding the subject area. Indeed, many of those interviewed expressed the view that employees across energy and nuclear energy institutions (not to mention the public) do not understand all the issues involved. They state that there is a shortage of current and prospective employees who can envisage the holistic picture of nuclear energy, and as a result organisations in the nuclear energy sector lack holistic decision-making ability. Therefore, decision-making on nuclear energy matters suffers from a piecemeal or fragmented approach: i.e. when a decision is made regarding a particular part of nuclear energy policy or regulation.

5.4   Energy law and policy development in the nuclear energy sector in the US: contested issues (hypotheses)

5.4.1   Hypothesis 1: State laws cannot effectively encourage or incentivise nuclear new build

The majority of research in the area states that nuclear policy is a national (Federal) issue in the US. Here the aim is to build on previous work by Parenteau (1976); Rabe (2004, 2006, 2007, 2008); Matisoff (2008); Mullin and Daley (2009); and Carley (2011), which identified the value of state laws where the Federal system does not provide direction. This is identified as being the case in the nuclear energy industry generally, and particularly regarding nuclear new build. It is shown that the state can have a considerable role in developing growth in new nuclear build. Hence, this research demonstrates the significant role of the state in the nuclear industry, despite the majority of the literature viewing the nuclear energy industry as a national or international industry.

The majority of the interviewees did not believe in the ability of state laws to affect or influence the nuclear new build policy. The view expressed by the majority was that it was at the Federal level that nuclear energy should be incentivised (CVP). There was the belief that it was not within a state's function, or remit, to be incentivising new energy infrastructure (CVP). Nevertheless, actions within Texas and Georgia demonstrate that there is the capability to incentivise or encourage new nuclear power plants. Following the assessment of the research analysis and the interview evidence, the hypothesis was unproven.

In Texas, many of the views supporting the hypothesis suggest a bias against nuclear energy. It was argued by many that even if the state has the capacity to incentivise nuclear power it should not do so, and it should support more natural gas and renewable energy (CVP). This bias, however, is demonstrated at an institutional level in Texas. For example, at state level Texas gives support to nuclear energy's competitors. Renewables, coal and natural gas all receive support (usually in the form of policy and subsequent financial subsidies through that policy) (TI-6). Renewable energy, in particular, receives heavy support in Texas due to its being considered a clean electricity source (TI-1, TI-2, TI-6, TI-10, TI-11). Yet the benefits of nuclear energy are not viewed in a similar way, despite the acceptance that: Texas needs energy supply diversity; there are benefits from keeping prices stable; and there is a need to move towards the goal of energy independence (TI-1, TI-2).

Those who support this hypothesis have several objections to nuclear receiving incentivisation at state level in Texas (CVP). First, nuclear energy is supported at Federal level and should remain so and the state legislature should not be concerned with it (CVP). This view is particularly prevalent with the development of the deregulated electricity market in Texas, where prices and competition mean that nuclear energy is too expensive and not an attractive option. Second, it is argued that nuclear energy has received subsidy support in the past, and it needs to be a financially independent industry now (CVP). Third, there is not the ability within the state to support nuclear energy due to the financial position of the state of Texas, which had a budget deficit of circa $6 billion for 2010 (Texas Comptroller of Public Accounts 2010).

These latter arguments are heard in Pennsylvania too, yet there are problems with these arguments in many cases. For example, deregulated markets have had problems in Texas and Pennsylvania, and no guarantees can be made that the introduction of nuclear energy would increase the price above what it may rise to in any case (CVC). There is no reason for the nuclear industry to be an independently financed industry, when its competitors are not (CVC) – more on subsidies will be discussed later. A state may have a budget deficit, but it can introduce other policies which could benefit nuclear energy but do not involve direct transfers of financial aid (CVC).

Critics of the hypothesis, who believe that state action can encourage nuclear, point to other policies that can occur without direct financial transfers. In Texas, these include encouraging regulated parts of the state to join together through incentives to develop a nuclear project, and applying some level of carbon tax (green tax), or giving nuclear energy the same benefits as renewables in the state (TI-1). Further, in both Texas and Pennsylvania attempts have been made to designate nuclear energy as a clean energy source and include it under their respective Renewable Portfolio Standards (RPS) (CVC). The latter is particularly emphasised by those in Texas who believe that the state is reaching its near maximum renewable capacity because of the massive investment in wind power (which is expected to continue), which has occurred due to the RPS and Senate Bill 20. Hence, if Texas is to continue to reduce its greenhouse gas (GHG) emissions, other clean energy projects will need to begin (CVC). Senate Bill 184 aims to initiate and support 'strategies for reducing greenhouse gas emissions that result in net savings for Texas consumers or businesses; can be achieved without financial cost to consumers or businesses; or help businesses in Texas maintain global competitiveness' (Senate Bill 184, p. 1). However, support for nuclear energy capable of reducing GHGs through the aims of Senate Bill 184 has yet to occur; nevertheless, it demonstrates that state-level policy has the capacity to encourage nuclear energy.

In Georgia, state laws have encouraged and even incentivised nuclear to some degree. There is a very strong pro-nuclear lobby in Georgia, and that lobby has assisted in the creation of the law there (CVC). A reason to create favourable laws in Georgia for nuclear energy lies in the risks of nuclear construction (GI-2, GI-4).[1] Georgia had in the past experienced such a situation where the cost escalated from \$3.214 billion (at 2007 US dollar currency equivalent) at the Edwin I Hatch nuclear power plant for two reactors (876MW and 883MW) completed in 1974, to \$19.071 billion (at 2007 USD currency) at the Plant Vogtle nuclear power plant for two reactors (1150MW and 1152MW), completed in 1989 (Energy Information Administration 2010).

It is recognised across public institutions in Georgia that the state needs to develop its energy mix and all forms of electricity will be supported should sufficient proposals be put forward (GI-1, GI-2). Nevertheless, legislation does support nuclear energy. One of the key pieces of legislation that favours nuclear energy at state level is Bill 31, which enacted the Georgia Nuclear Energy Financing Act. This permits the state utility, Georgia Power, to recover the costs of construction from the beginning of the construction phase – these are known as Construction Work In Progress (CWIP) payments. This legislation was only introduced in 2009. An earlier form of the legislation was in fact drafted and attempts were made to introduce it in 1974–5; however, this was rejected. Now the new law is not to favour nuclear as such, but to realise within the electricity sector '. . . what's needed, what capacity has got to be out there, what the environmental impact is going to be, we have to make leadership decisions and make those decisions, (that) maybe (are) not political, but factually we think . . . better' (GI-2).

The research thus identifies, through the policy actions in all three states, the first lesson of the research, that:

Lesson 1: *State laws in the US do indeed have the capacity to encourage and incentivise nuclear new build.*

5.4.2 Hypothesis 2: Deregulation of the electricity sector in US states has not succeeded

Deregulation of electricity markets has occurred across the European Union and the US. The rate at, and extent to, which it has occurred are different. In the US, twenty-five states have not deregulated their electricity markets. According to the academic literature (Joskow 2005; Slocum 2008; Blumsack 2007), the success of deregulation in the US is mixed. This corresponds to the views of those interviewed. The hypothesis was proven after the evidence from the research analysis demonstrated that deregulation in the two US states has not succeeded, and the resulting analysis that follows testifies to this.

Opinion is evenly contested on average across the three US states concerning deregulation. However, in Georgia it does not present itself as an issue at state level due to it being a regulated state, and significantly there were no calls to deregulate the electricity market from the respondents. Texas and Pennsylvania provide interesting contrasts in examining electricity deregulation in the US. Texas has its own grid system, ERCOT, and within this system there are also regulated and unregulated areas, while Pennsylvania shares a grid, PJM, which now covers thirteen states and the District of Columbia.

Deregulation was introduced through legislation in Texas in 1999 (Senate Bill 7) and began in 2002. Deregulation was brought into Texas with the promise of increasing economic efficiency in the electricity supply sector, reducing the cost, and therefore prices to consumers. However, as the state sought lower prices, deregulation and its long-term effects on the entire electricity industry were not considered (CVP). Deregulation has performed one main role in Texas, and that is to offer consumers more choice about where they purchase electricity. However, there is a list of non-achievements (CVP). There is no evidence that it has delivered new generation, new transmission or reduced electricity prices (CVP). The new electricity generation in Texas that has occurred has only been because of very generous wind subsidies introduced by subsequent legislation that masks the cost of wind (CVP). Poor investment in new transmission structures still inhibits the addition of new generation as well as the performance of existing generation facilities (TI-1, TI-2, TI-6, TI-15). Further, prices have not decreased for consumers in the deregulated areas of Texas, which suffer in particular from natural gas price volatility and, consequently, electricity prices have become some of the most expensive in the US (CVP). Electricity prices are, however, lower in the regulated parts of the state than the deregulated parts (TI-6, TI-11). This explains the reluctance of the regulated parts of the state of Texas to deregulate. Incidentally, some of the municipalities that remain regulated are involved in both the nuclear projects in Texas: the South Texas Project and Comanche Peak. This represents a similarity to Georgia, in identifying that new nuclear build can happen in regulated electricity markets.

In Pennsylvania, a similar evolution of the electricity market has occurred following deregulation. Again, however, the introduction of deregulation has been criticised by interviewees (PI-1, PI-2, PI-4, PI-5, PI-13). It is reported that legislation was introduced to improve market prices and did not have new electricity generation or environmental concerns at its core (CVP). The actions by those in public administration institutions for the electricity industry were incomplete (CVP). A new policy (deregulation was enacted in 1998) was introduced in the electricity market without considering its long-term effects or the evolution of the industry (CVP). Renewable energy was also given heavy subsidies through the later introduction of a Renewable Portfolio Standard in Pennsylvania. Those who believe in market deregulation within the state believe that the new market system needs to be given more time, and that PJM needs to develop as an institution (PI-8, PI-9, PI-10).

The majority of interviewees across the three states believe that deregulation has not succeeded, though some take the view in relation to this that the expectations of deregulation were unrealistic or over-optimistic. This (despite the influence of the Georgia results) highlights the need for a revision of the deregulation policy in these states. Blumsack (2007) examined the restructuring process in the US and stated that it is unclear whether electricity deregulation in the USA is a success or failure. Notably, he stated (2007: 183–4):

> If electricity restructuring in the United States fails, it is not because of Enron or any other group of stakeholders, but rather because the markets and institutions emerged from a poor formulation of the problem that restructuring was supposed to solve. California's doomed market was designed without sufficient input from experienced engineers; by default this yielded an incomplete set of performance metrics and a verification process somewhere between terrible and nonexistent. The current controversy over regional integration in markets and electric grids stems from a lack of clarity regarding the policy goals underlying restructuring. Whether lower prices for consumers, open access to transmission, or the promotion of markets itself is the ultimate goal is far from clear. Just as problematic as the lack of well-defined policy goals is the lack of well-defined metrics for verifying whether the policy goals have been met. Good metrics are objective, thorough, consensual, and are reflected in policy decisions.

A return to regulated electricity markets may not be the way forward, but some interviewees identified the need for electricity markets which had environmental policy and development of infra-structure as major considerations (PI-2, PI-4, PI-10, PI-11, PI-12,

PI-13). States developed electricity policy in isolation from their other policies such as environmental policy, when electricity policy needs to be developed in unison (or at least in coordination) with other state policies (CVP). Focusing on short-term objectives (or electricity prices in the short term) was not the path forward, and the increase in electricity prices post-deregulation is evidence of the need for a new review of the deregulation process (CVP).

The evidence demonstrates three major policy issues: first, that the plans and strategies for the creation of these deregulated markets were ill-defined from the outset and this problem has not yet been resolved; second, that the electricity industry is an example where market liberalisation policies have not delivered; and third, the push for deregulation shows a conflict with considerable tension between states' attempts to manage their economies, environments and financial resources. These latter three issues and the research analysis into the contested hypothesis identify two lessons learned from this hypothesis for the future:

> Lesson 2: *The public administration system in the electricity sector at state level in the US would benefit from realigning policy instruments with the policy goals of the sector.*
>
> Lesson 3: *Deregulation as a policy in the electricity sector at state level merits a review.*

5.4.3   Hypothesis 3: Nuclear energy is an underfunded sector within the electricity sector

The views of the respondents are nearly evenly divided across the three states on the issue. 'Underfunded' in this hypothesis is taken to refer to funding or finance from state or Federal institutional sources. With opinion divided, it is evident that there is at some level a lack of information dissemination on the financial health of the nuclear energy sector. This represents a key concern for an industry such as nuclear energy, where finance is an important issue because of high nuclear project costs and where safety issues are paramount.

The majority of the literature on nuclear energy policy in relation to finance is dominated by nuclear economics and where construction costs are to the fore (Cantor and Hewlett 1988; Mooz 1978, 1979; Paik and Schriver 1979; Komanoff 1981; Zimmerman 1982; Applied

Decision Analysis 1983; Navarro 1988; Proops 2001; Massachusetts Institute of Technology 2003, 2009). This research aims to focus more on the subsidies available to the industry and the financing of initiatives to encourage confidence in the industry (such as through safety and educational initiatives).

Some previous research has stated that the nuclear industry receives too many subsidies, such as through the Price-Anderson Act that provides a limited compensation fund of $10 billion should there be a nuclear accident (Dubin and Rothwell 1990). The majority of interviewees were of the same belief and against the hypothesis. Nevertheless, the research into the hypothesis provides evidence contrary to that view: for example, underfunded safety initiatives in Georgia and subsidies in the electricity sector in Texas. Following the assessment of the research analysis and the interview evidence of the minority, Hypothesis 3 was determined as proven, as the rest of this section will demonstrate.

Pennsylvania

Pennsylvania represents a different case from the other two states regarding this hypothesis, yet the hypothesis is similarly contested across all three states. Funding for state initiatives in the nuclear sector after the Three Mile Island (TMI) accident was of paramount importance to the state legislature in Pennsylvania (PI-7, PI-8, PI-10). State agencies received increased and sufficient levels of funding (PI-7, PI-8). Nuclear energy is seen as a vital part of the economy in Pennsylvania, and counteracts the environmental pollution from coal, and, despite TMI, people are accepting of nuclear energy in the state (PI-1, PI-4, PI-5, PI-7, PI-8, PI-10).

In Pennsylvania, despite the attention given to adequate funding for state agencies in the nuclear sector, too much is expected of the private sector in terms of its ability to disseminate information to the public who need to be better informed (CVP). In particular, this function (formerly one of the public sector before privatisation) has not transferred itself to the private sector as yet (PI-4, PI-13, PI-14, PI-15). Two issues are analysed here which demonstrate this same issue in the other two states. One concerns Texas, where people have a view that the nuclear energy sector is not underfunded. The other example is from Georgia, where the funding of a safety initiative identifies the lack of transparency in information provision in the sector.

Texas

The first issue regarding subsidy levels raises the problem of misinformation concerning subsidy levels in the electricity sector. In the case of the electricity sector, there is the need for a proper evaluation of subsidy levels and the merits of those levels. Competition in the electricity sector, particularly as the example that follows from Texas will demonstrate, is unfairly balanced (CVP). If deregulation of the electricity markets was an aim of the Texas state legislature, then this issue should have been resolved, as otherwise some incumbents and subsidised newcomers can emerge in stronger industry positions (CVP). There was a lack of research into how to level the 'playing field' for different electricity firms (CVP). This is not to mention which sources of electricity should have been preferred so as to benefit other state policies (i.e. so as to improve the state environmental policy or decrease carbon emissions). This demonstrates an example where best practice in the public administration process of deregulation could have been achieved.

Nuclear energy is considered by many of those interviewed (CVP) as an expensive option for electricity production for a variety of reasons. This centres on the industry having long construction times, being a highly complex technical project, and having extensive safety and environmental regulatory regimes. In addition, other interviewees (CVC) attached significant budget overruns and subsidies to nuclear projects. However, a few interviewees expressed the view that it is the uncertainty of what subsidies are available to nuclear energy that is adding to its expense (TI-12, TI-13). If there were the potential to cost nuclear to an accurate level, there would be more movement by individual firms to build new nuclear.

As stated, the lack of information dissemination is a feature of the nuclear energy industry, and across the energy industry itself in relation to subsidies. Nuclear energy is often challenged as an industry which is in receipt of too many subsidies (CVP). However, all across the energy industry subsidies are an everyday *modus operandi*. Indeed, while it is difficult to calculate subsidies (both direct and indirect) received by source when environmental factors are taken into

Table 5.2 Subsidies for different energy sources

Energy type	Subsidy estimate (US$ billion/year)	Subsidies per energy unit (US cents/kWh)
Nuclear energy	45	1.7
Renewable energy (excluding hydroelectricity)	27	5.0
Biofuels	20	5.1
Fossil fuels	400	0.8

Source: Relative subsidies to energy sources, Global Subsidies Initiative, 2010

account, Arias and van Beers (2010) demonstrate in a review of cal-culated subsidies that fossil fuels have been in receipt of major subsi-dies in industrialised nations. Further, a global assessment of subsidies in the energy sector as shown in Table 5.2 demonstrates that fossil fuels still receive significant subsidies, and this figure is unquestionably higher according to an International Energy Institute (2010) report which stated that globally it was €550 billion in 2008.

Table 5.3 details at a Federal level the estimated amount each fuel source receives as a share in the total amount of subsidies ($13.6 billion) coming from the Federal government. The data demonstrates that nuclear energy receives only 8.7 per cent, while coal (20.2 per cent), oil and gas (25.7 per cent) receive a significant share of the subsidies. Yet it is nuclear energy that has the major reputation for receiving subsidies (CVP).

In examining the subsidies at state level for the electricity sector, Table 5.4 demonstrates that nuclear receives no subsidies while the oil and gas sector receives $1.4 billion. Yet the majority of interview-ees are unaware of such subsidies to nuclear's competitors in the electricity sector in Texas. These levels of subsidies in Table 5.3 and Table 5.4 demonstrate that, while nuclear energy does receive subsidies at the Federal level, it receives less than its major competitors in Texas, such as gas and coal, and it receives distinctly less at state

Table 5.3 Estimated percentages of Federal subsidies for different fuel sources in 2006 in the US

Energy source	Percentage share
Ethanol	34.6
Oil and gas	25.7
Coal	20.2
Nuclear	8.7
Wind	3.4
Solar	2.8
Hydroelectric	2.2
Biomass	1.5
Biodiesel	0.7
Geothermal	0.2

Total Federal subsidies: $13.6 billion

Source: Adapted by the author from Texas Comptroller of Public Accounts, 'Energy Report 2008', p. 371

Table 5.4 Estimated Texas state and local taxpayer subsidies in 2006

Energy source	Texas state and local subsidies	Energy source	Texas state and local subsidies
Oil and Gas	$1,417,434,337	Ethanol	n/a
Coal	n/a	Biodiesel	$2,107,420
Nuclear	n/a	Wind	$1,508,800
Total	$1,417,434,337	Solar	$2,574,101*
		Hydroelectric	n/a
		Biomass	n/a
		Geothermal	$45,400
		Total	$6,235,721

n/a = not applicable
*$2,074,101 of this total comes from Austin Energy utility company.

Source: Compiled by the author from Texas Comptroller of Public Accounts, 'Energy Report 2008', p. 372

level. Indeed, gas receives nearly $1.1 billion in severance tax incentives, in particular for high-cost oil wells.

Georgia
The second issue concerns the financing of safety and education initiatives in industry. It is discussed how, at a time of planned industry expansion, costs were being reduced in safety and education initiatives. Elements of the nuclear power programme are underfunded in Georgia (GI-9). Expressed through the interviews, this is not just the view of the Southern Alliance for Clean Energy environmental group. This latter organisation, however, has taken Southern Nuclear to court in order to secure more transparency in the operations of Southern Nuclear on their nuclear activities (GI-9).

Despite the ambition of Southern Nuclear to develop more nuclear power, it cannot ignore some of the financial concerns faced by other institutions in the state which affect those institutions' performance of their duties to high standards of safety. For example, the Environmental Protection Division (EPD), which operates the Environmental Radiation Program (ERP), has suffered financial cuts at a time when the nuclear industry is proposing expansion in Georgia (GI-5). Upon closer examination, it is Southern Nuclear that has contributed funding to this agency. It also made funding cutbacks to this agency over the period 2007–10, despite this period also representing the time when it was actively promoting its nuclear new build expansion plans (GI-5). However, the latter company did not act in isolation and the state legislator had a role to play too; and, according to an employee at the Environmental Radiation Program:

> We've had some instances in the past just with our programme where there were proposals that would have threatened the existence of this programme. And the way I've heard it . . . Southern Company legislators or lobbyists came to our aid and made sure that the legislature knew that if they carried through the proposals that they were talking about, that it would . . . in doing harm to our programme in effect harm them as well. (GI-5)

It is clear that there is a realisation by Southern Nuclear, lobbyists and the legislature (the state of Georgia) that funding is needed for environmental programmes. However, despite this Southern Nuclear still persisted in reducing their funding. With work having already started at the site in Georgia by Southern Nuclear 2009 under a Limited Work Authorization permit, this action was inconsistent with the aim of nuclear expansion. It demonstrates poor public management in the state of Georgia that it has not prioritised safety in the electricity sector in new electricity generation projects.

In Georgia, those interviewees who are proponents of the hypothesis (CVP) state that there is a lack of understanding of the nuclear energy sector in the context of there not being the realisation that the composite parts of the nuclear energy sector make up the whole. For example, prioritising funding – which in the case of the EPD-EPR agency is a fraction of an overall nuclear budget – for such small but vital agencies that can increase public confidence in the nuclear sector represents good public management practice. It would demonstrate that those in nuclear sector have safety at the forefront of their operations and policy. In Georgia, this should be of particular relevance due to the presence on the River Keowee of reactors in South Carolina which have had bad reports concerning leaks of radioactive waste into the water (GI-5). This is in contrast to the performance of the Vogtle reactors on the same river where – not accounting for batch releases, which are a normal process in the nuclear energy process – monitoring on the Vogtle plant has revealed no accidental or major releases, and that 'you'd have a hard time proving from our environmental monitoring results that there were nuclear plants there' (GI-5). This latter view, and the scientific analysis that supports it, need to be disseminated to the public in Georgia: i.e. the environmental monitoring results of this agency need to be publicised to demonstrate part of the environmental record of the operation of Plant Vogtle (GI-5). This could encourage public support for nuclear activities. Instead, this agency has insufficient funds to do so, nor are the value of its activities realised by other organisations in the Georgia nuclear sector (GI-4, GI-5, GI-9).

The analysis of the hypothesis revealed two major concerns over information dissemination in the nuclear industry, concerning subsidy levels, and the level of financing of safety and educational initiatives.

This highlights the lessons learned in the nuclear energy sector for the future from the analysis of this hypothesis:

Lesson 4: *Policies for further information dissemination should be facilitated in the electricity sector at US state level.*

Lesson 5: *Consideration should be given to the establishment of new state-level agencies which can disseminate information on the electricity industry and in particular on the financial health of safety and educational initiatives.*

5.4.4 Hypothesis 4: There is no nuclear renaissance in the US

This hypothesis was contested on average across the states. The majority of those interviewed believed that there is no nuclear renaissance in the US. However, despite this, and a low number of critics, after the research analysis into the hypothesis, it was not proven.

The hypothesis was not proven for a number of reasons. The analysis demonstrates that there is a misconception of the nuclear renaissance, and what it was expected to be. Further, there has been a failure to take into account the evolution of the nuclear industry. Indeed, academic literature has recognised these issues (Joskow and Baughman 1976; Rossin and Rieck 1978; Kasperson et al. 1980: Lester 1986). The nuclear industry is still growing in the US, albeit at a much slower pace than in the 1960s and 1970s. Indeed, its market penetration for a new technology was significant – circa 20 per cent of the electricity market. This same level of market penetration should not have been expected to occur again, for the academic literature (see above, and Lund 2006) suggests that market penetration levels will decrease as market share rises. Therefore, the expectation for the nuclear sector would be slow incremental growth rather than a significant increase in the growth rate. This research aims to build upon this previous literature.

The nuclear industry has entered a new phase of evolution. This consists of plant upgrades (uprates) and licence renewals for existing nuclear reactors, which have resulted in the slow regeneration of the industry. Indeed, one of the major developments in the nuclear industry over the 1990–2010 period was the upgrades to nuclear reactors. The EIA (2010) has stated that year-on-year nuclear capacity has increased each year from about 0.2 per cent to 0.4 per cent due to uprates in existing plants. There are, however, two other developments that may have affected the evolution of the sector. A number of the interviewees who were proponents of the hypothesis stated that the nuclear renaissance was not going to happen and, if it were to have happened, it would have been at a more advanced stage by now. However, to propound that view is to ignore two fundamental characteristics of the nuclear energy industry which will be discussed in the following paragraphs: (1) the technologically determined attributes of the nuclear industry; and (2) the fact that the pace of change in the industry is defined by lengthy regulation and legal hearing processes. These characteristics are not unique to the US.

Technologically determined attributes of the nuclear industry
The change in technology in the nuclear industry concerns two effects: (1) the ability to prolong in operation the existing technology; and (2) the next generation reactor technology to be employed at new nuclear power plants in the US.

The majority of existing nuclear power plants can be expected to receive twenty-year licence renewals in addition to their initial forty-year licenses (based on the fact that seventy out of the 104 reactors in the US have already been granted renewals – NRC 2010). Maintaining this assumption will mean that a third of the existing US nuclear energy capacity will close between 2029 and 2035.[2] However, applying for a licence to operate a nuclear power plant beyond sixty years is not out of the question (CVC). It should be recalled that the Atomic Energy Act of 1954 authorised the US NRC to issue operating licenses for commercial nuclear power plants for a period of forty years.[3] This forty-year time frame was not based upon technical limitations, but accounting and antitrust concerns (Nuclear Regulatory Commission 2007). The law permits the NRC to issue operating licence renewals in twenty-year increments, provided that the reactor owners demonstrate that continued operations can be conducted safely. As of 2009, the NRC has granted licence renewals to fifty of the 104 US reactors. Fifteen applications are under review and another twenty-one operators have indicated their intention to apply.[4] So far, no applications have been refused. In December 2009 the Oyster Creek Generating Station in New Jersey became the first nuclear reactor to begin its fortieth year of operation, so it will be another five or ten years before there is an indication of whether to continue beyond sixty years, provided that extending the life of a reactor remains an economically viable route.

Technological development has also occurred in the provision of new reactors. Nuclear new build projects in the US will all use Generation III technology – similar to current projects in France and Finland. In essence, the industry is rejuvenating itself, as it is undergoing an evolutionary phase to the next technological stage, and this is a slow process rather than a rapid one (CVC). This argument is further augmented by the changes which the regulator (NRC) has introduced into the industry in applying for design approval. New incentives for nuclear power (but not limited to nuclear power) were also introduced with the Federal Energy Policy Act of 2005; however, they have been slow to be implemented into the industry. For example, it was fully six years later, in 2011, that the first loan guarantees were awarded – in this case to Georgia (Southern Nuclear). Nevertheless, since 2005 firms in the nuclear energy sector have been developing their plans (CVC); Plant Vogtle in Georgia will be the first to go through the new regulation process, which consists of a Combined Operating and Licensing system (COL). The nuclear plant was issued a Limited Work Authorization permit in 2009, and was also successful in securing an Early Site Permit (ESP) in 2009. It then applied for the COL, and this was awarded finally in February 2012. A COL was also awarded to the VC Summer nuclear plant in the neighbouring state of South Carolina in March 2012, while Tennessee Valley Authority are pushing to finish nuclear reactors where construction had previously stopped in the 1980s at Watts Bar Unit 2 and Bellefonte.

The pace of change in the industry is defined by lengthy regulatory hearing processes

Little has changed since the last period when nuclear new build projects began construction (CVP). Public administration has not improved in terms of delivering a coherent long-term energy policy (CVP). Nuclear energy is cited as being one of the solutions in the battle against climate change, and also for US energy security and

US energy independence (CVP). However, to date this has not been supported at an administrative level. The Energy Policy Act of 2005 (the '2005 Act') which incentivised nuclear new build, and was responsible for eight applications for nuclear new build projects, has been slow in its implementation: 'it [the 2005 Act] has taken years to implement' (FNI-7). It was only in 2011 that the first company was awarded loan guarantees under the 2005 Act, and the amount stated to be available under the loan guarantee system has been demonstrated to have been significantly too low. This is evidenced by the 2005 Act, which allowed for $18.5 billion for loan guarantees; however, the Georgia project has claimed nearly half of these ($8.33 billion). Further, the Obama administration has debated and sought unsuccessfully an increase to the amount available under the loan guarantee system of up to $36 billion in 2010 (Chu 2010) and $54.5 billion in 2011 (Holt 2011).

Mechanisms to deliver on policy in the form of outcomes remain a weakness of the US public administration system. Nor are there examples of project management for large infrastructure projects having improved in the US (TI-15). The NRC, viewed as a contributor to the time delays and cost overruns in the last nuclear new build projects, has aimed to standardise the design process for new projects, and implemented the new COL licensing process in order to decrease the length of time of the licensing process and provide more certainty in the process to potential operators (CVP). However, it is a new process, and Southern Nuclear in Georgia is the first company to go through this new regulatory regime; consequently, as the test case, the process is expected to be slower (CVP).

The lessons learned from this hypothesis were:

Lesson 6: *Uncertainty in the legal structure of the nuclear industry continues to be a factor that hinders new investment. A legal system that establishes more confidence should be encouraged.*

Lesson 7: *The nuclear energy project in Georgia is a test case of the current legal regime and the lessons learned from this test case need to be implemented quickly to encourage future nuclear new build.*

Lesson 8: *The impact of electricity laws, such as the Energy Policy Act of 2005, would benefit from re-examination in light of the slow implementation process of these Acts.*

5.5   Conclusion

This research identifies key lessons over the period 1990–2010 from the nuclear energy sector which can enhance the conditions needed for new nuclear build. The research demonstrates the evolution of the nuclear industry in the US, which has taken the form of incremental change. The chapter advances research in nuclear energy policy in adding to the limited research that focuses in particular on nuclear new build. It contributes a three state study. While no nuclear new build occurred in the US over the period 1990–2010, the industry was nevertheless active. Capacity increased at existing nuclear plants, licences to extend reactor lifetimes were applied for and plans were firmly developed in Georgia for two units at an existing facility (Plant Vogtle). However, as the industry was on the verge of a nuclear new build project for the first time in this period, the research identifies a number of policy areas that would facilitate growth of the sector should they be reviewed. The research provides these new insights through a unique comparison of US states which have deregulated, regulated and 'hybrid' electricity markets.

The research also advances knowledge in the public administration of the electricity sector, and in particular contributes to the literature on state-led policy action within the US. The research identifies that any overall review of state energy policies would (or at least could) be beneficial to nuclear energy, due to it also being a source of clean energy. Primarily, this concerns electricity deregulation policy and information provision on the sector. Deregulation as a policy in the electricity sector is in need of reform in some states. It has failed to provide for investment in the transmission system or new generation, and prices have not decreased. The lack of information dissemination in the nuclear energy sector is expressed as a major concern that is yet to be resolved. Consideration should be given to the establishment of a new state-level agency which can disseminate information on the electricity industry, and in particular on the financial health of safety and education initiatives in the nuclear energy sector.

Numerous legal conditions have changed in the nuclear energy sector which increase the likelihood of future nuclear new build. In this context, the research builds upon and advances the literature that focuses on the legal development of the energy sector. From the research it is evident that law can play a central role in the nuclear energy sector. State legislatures have become more active in the electricity sector and there is potential for them to incentivise nuclear projects at a local level. The Nuclear Regulatory Commission has re-designed the construction and operating licence system, which was previously a cause of delay. Nevertheless, the nuclear energy project in Georgia is a test case of the current legal regime and the lessons learned from this test case need to be implemented quickly to encourage future nuclear new build. Uncertainty in the legal structure of the nuclear industry continues to be one of the factors that hinders new investment and needs to be reviewed. In this regard, the impact and the evolution of electricity law (such as the Energy Policy Act of 2005) should be re-examined in light of its slow implementation process.

Although this research focused on nuclear energy policy in the USA from 1990 to 2010, and thus pre-dates the nuclear energy crisis at Fukushima in Japan in March 2011, nevertheless the lessons to improve the conditions for future nuclear new build in the US still remain valid, if not even more important. This is because the accident at Fukushima subjects the US nuclear industry to even more scrutiny. The nuclear project in Georgia will serve the industry as the test case. In all likelihood, the onus or burden of proof will fall on the nuclear industry, ever more so, to prove its credentials in terms of meeting its operating safety requirements and having the capability to build a project to the highest safety standards as well as on time and on budget.

Exploring Energy Policy Inaction and Contradiction: The Case of Nuclear Energy in the US, 1990–2010

6.1 Introduction

This chapter examines, from a policy perspective, US Federal policy inaction and contradiction in the nuclear energy sector from 1990 to 2010. Several examples at the Federal level are identified which demonstrate that the nuclear industry has evolved to a stage where it requires a focus on the power of actions at a more localised (state) level in order to re-ignite the industry.

The chapter concludes that there remains a misunderstanding of the issue of project management for complex construction projects, and it is highly arguable whether many of the issues involved have been resolved. Further, the economics of nuclear energy are not the most influential reason for the absence of nuclear new build in the US. The chapter highlights a review of the nuclear renaissance in the US, which concludes that the renaissance had not already transpired by 2010; hence, the impact of Fukushima in the context of nuclear new build in the US was limited.

6.2 Brief background to the US electricity and nuclear industries

Civilian nuclear energy accounts for 22 per cent of the total electricity supply in the US (see Table 6.1). There are 104 nuclear reactors across the US, representing a quarter of the total number of nuclear reactors in the world. The nuclear power industry in the US grew to its present capacity primarily through the construction programmes initiated during the 1960s and 1970s.

Renewable energy is playing a growing role in the US electricity market. Renewable energy sources are projected to have the

Table 6.1 Electricity generated by source in the US, 2009

Supply source	Share of electricity generated by source (%)
Petroleum	1%
Natural gas	18%
Coal	48%
Renewable energy	11%
Nuclear	22%

Source: Compiled by the author from the Energy Information Administration (EIA) Annual Energy Review 2009 (EIA 2010b)

strongest growth over the medium term due to Federal and state level programmes – such as the Federal Renewable Fuels Standard (RFS) and the various State Renewable Portfolio Standards (RPS) programmes – and the rise in fossil fuel prices. In some projections, renewables will account for 45 per cent of the increase in total generation from 2008 to 2035 (Energy Information Administration 2010a).

Nevertheless, despite many reactor closures (twenty-three reactors have been permanently shut down (Nuclear Regulatory Commission 2011)) and no new nuclear build, nuclear energy maintained its position in the US electricity market in the period 1990–2010 owing to the better utilisation of generating capacity, uprates and life extensions (see Table 6.2).

Reactors are located at sixty-five sites (plants) in the US, with the majority of plants located in the eastern half of the country in thirty-three states. Sixty-nine of the reactors in operation are pressurised water reactors, and thirty-five are boiling water reactors.

The analysis that follows is based in part on the responses of those interviewed for the research. In the text analysis that follows, interview statements attributed to interviewees are in codes (with a number corresponding to the interviewee's category of institution, and a letter to their specific institution; see the tables in the Appendix for more information). Further, some statements are supported by a majority view of critics or proponents of the hypothesis and in these cases the

Table 6.2 Licence renewals and power uprates in the US nuclear sector

Licence renewals		Power uprates	
Total reactors in the US	104	Power uprates	Number and electricity added
Licence renewal granted	71	Granted	139 and 5,960.7 MWe
Under review	14	Under review	10 and 1,335 MWe
Expected future applications	15	Expected future applications (2011–15)	35 and 1,855 MWe

Source: Compiled by the author as of October 2011 from Nuclear Regulatory Commission statistics (2011)

reference code is either CVP (the Consensus View of Proponents), or CVC (Consensus View of the Critics).

6.3 Energy law and policy inaction in the US: contested issues (hypotheses)

6.3.1 Hypothesis 1: Federal laws favour the development of the nuclear energy sector

This hypothesis is near evenly contested between those interviewed. There is a slight majority against the hypothesis. The view expressed by the hypothesis proponents was that it was at the Federal level that nuclear energy should be incentivised (CVP). There was also a belief that it was not within a state's function, or remit, to incentivise new energy infrastructure (CVP). Nevertheless, actions within a number of states demonstrate that there exists the capability to incentivise or encourage new nuclear power plants. The research analysis that follows demonstrates the inaction at Federal level and the effect on state policy, and hence this contested hypothesis is unproven.

The hypothesis has not been proven for four main reasons. First, the Energy Policy Act of 2005 was meant to re-ignite the industry, and has so far failed to have a significant influence (CVC). Second, critics of the hypothesis argue that there is a misconception that the Energy Policy Act of 2005 was created to benefit nuclear (CVC). Third, while the Nuclear Regulatory Commission (NRC) has improved as an institution, it has achieved this improvement from a very low base (CVP). Finally, at a Federal level in nuclear energy issues there is a general state of policy inaction.

The major legislation in the civil nuclear energy sector in the US
The centrepiece of nuclear legislation in the US is the Atomic Energy Act of 1954 (42 USC 2011 et seq.), a comprehensive Federal statute that regulates possession and use of radioactive material and facilities that produce or use such material. There are also several other statutes that cover more specific aspects of the regulation of radioactive material and facilities, for example, in radiological protection, radiological waste management, non-proliferation, exports and nuclear security.

To recap (see section 5.3 of this volume), other key laws in the nuclear energy sector are:

• Energy Reorganisation Act of 1974
• Department of Energy Organisation Act of 1977
• Nuclear Waste Policy Act 1982
• The Energy Policy Act of 2005
• Price-Anderson Act of 1957.

The misconception about who benefits from the Energy Policy Act of 2005
The Energy Policy of Act 2005 (hereafter also referred to as the '2005 Act') has been significant for nuclear energy in terms of the incentives it has offered but has not yet delivered any for nuclear new build. A key incentive offered is through the loan guarantee system (see section 3.2 for the extended earlier discussion). The 2005 Act allowed for $18.5 billion for loan guarantees, with the Georgia project claiming $6.5 billion. It is likely that only two to three projects will be able to use the loan guarantee system, and it is because of this that the Obama administration debated and sought (unsuccessfully) an increase of up

to $36 billion in 2010 (Chu 2010) and $54.5 billion in 2011 (Holt 2011).

Nuclear energy was not the only energy sector to receive subsidy support through loan guarantees under the 2005 Act. Table 6.3 below shows that incentives were given to all energy sectors. Gas and oil received subsidies of various types, and in particular the permit process was shortened to deliver quicker supplies of oil and gas (ss. 265, 366). Renewables and coal (CCS technology) also received a subsidy through the form of the loan guarantee system. CCS technology has also received further subsidies through the American Recovery and Reinvestment Act of 2009 (Pu. L. No. 115–5). Despite the loan guarantee system having been established under the 2005 Act for all clean energy sources (non-carbon dioxide emitting electricity sources), the same negative publicity received by the nuclear sector regarding the loan system has not been received by the renewable energy and coal CCS technology industries (CVC).

Furthermore, critics of the hypothesis state that there is, in particular, a misguided notion of exactly what the loan guarantee system entails (CVC). There is a view that this is a Federal subsidy. However, it is a subsidy for which the industry is paying itself. Among those who are entitled to the loan guarantee system within the clean energy sector (non-carbon dioxide emitting sources), it is only in the nuclear energy sector that project sponsors must pay a subsidy cost. This latter cost is the estimated average by the government of the future cost from defaulted loans in the loan guarantee system. This can have an impact on the viability of a project if it is too high, as it adds another significant cost to the overall project cost – for example, if the rate were 10 per cent, or indeed the 11.8 per cent ($880 million) quoted to Constellation Energy for the Calvert Cliff project (Wallace 2010). Arguably, therefore, it is not the subsidy that others claim (CVP).

The Price-Anderson Act, however, was renewed for a further twenty years by the Energy Policy Act of 2005. This Act does seem to benefit nuclear energy, in particular in the light of the BP Deepwater Horizon oil spill in 2010. Under the Oil Pollution Act of 1990 oil companies are only liable for $75 million, yet BP was obliged to make available $20 billion and pay its own costs associated with the disaster (estimated to be nearly $3 billion) (National Commission 2011). Risk and the financial amount stated in the Price-Anderson

Table 6.3 Selection of incentives from the Energy Policy Act of 2005

Issue	Incentive offered
Construction risk (s. 638)	Offers risk assurance to cover 100 per cent of delays (up to $500 million) for the first two nuclear plants and 50 per cent of delays (up to $250 million) for plants three to six.
Insurance (Title VI, Subtitle A)	Extends the Price-Anderson Act that applies to the civil nuclear energy sector for a further twenty years.
Loan guarantee system (Title XVII)	Creation of new loan guarantee office for any clean energy technologies. Authorises loan guarantee (up to 80 per cent of project cost for nuclear) but also for IGCC (Integrated gasification combined cycle) plants and renewable energy projects, hydrogen fuel cell technology, carbon capture and sequestration projects, and the construction of refineries for gasoline, ethanol and biodiesel.
Production tax credits (s. 1306)	Production tax credit 1.8 cents per kilowatt-hour for 6,000 megawatts of capacity from nuclear power plants for the first eight years of operation. Wind and closed loop biomass have received a production tax credit since 1992 and received a further extension of this (s. 1301 for federal land projects).
Permit process (s. 365)	Permitting process for oil and gas was streamlined and this cuts out years and months of delays in a Western states pilot programme – it will bring new gas and oil to the market sooner. Section 366 even states it is possible for a permit to drill to be issued within thirty days – though this is for a pilot project across Western states only.

Source: Compiled by the author as of October 2011 from Nuclear Regulatory Commission statistics (2011)

Act may need to be re-examined in this light: however, this is an area of future research given that all financial data from the BP Horizon spill are not yet available for a full examination, with BP disputing the final amounts to be paid out in compensation.

The improvement of the Nuclear Regulatory Commission
The NRC has improved as an institution over the 1990–2010 period since its previous existence in the 1960s and 1970s (H-1). However, it must be stated that the NRC was improving from a poor performance level and there remains a need for further improvement (CVC). Prior poor performance can be attributed to the NRC having just been established as a new agency and facing the severe problem of the Three Mile Island accident almost immediately thereafter (FNI-5, FNI-6). However, despite no nuclear new build having been approved by the NRC under the new COL system, it has been active throughout the 1990s and 2000s. It has approved power upgrades licence renewals for many of the 104 reactors, as shown earlier in Table 6.2.

There is, however, recognition by the majority of respondents that the NRC can continue to improve and needs to do so if more projects are to begin (CVC). Improvements, according to those interviewed, should focus on three core areas. The NRC needs to: (1) become more predictable; (2) decrease the length of the licensing process; and (3) become more adaptable to change (CVC). For example, the NRC has to play a more active role in ensuring safety, and to address concerns that may arise from nuclear problems at other reactor sites across the world (CVC). Hence, there remains the need for further change at the NRC.

Policy inaction
Federal laws have over time become less effective in the nuclear energy sector, and this highlights the three issues analysed here. The Energy Policy Act of 2005 and its implementation need to be re-examined, and the NRC regulatory process needs to improve, including the development of a faster approval process.

At a Federal level, this policy inaction is also evident in the field of nuclear waste management, which is an issue that still remains unresolved (H-3). There is widespread agreement that one of the major obstacles to a nuclear revival is the management and storage of spent nuclear reactor fuel and other high-level radioactive waste (2A, 4A, 4E, 4F, 5B). According to the literature, the nuclear industry has concentrated on and solved many of its problems; however, it has not resolved this one.

The Nuclear Waste Policy Act 1982 initially scheduled a first repository site to be chosen by March 1987, with a second by March 1990. Neither requirement was met, but by 1989 Yucca Mountain had emerged as the choice. The 1987 Amendments to the Nuclear Waste Policy Act (NWPA) did, however, specifically state that the waste management programme would be at Yucca Mountain. Nevertheless, it was not until 2008 that a licence application was submitted to the NRC (Nuclear Regulatory Commission 2008), before being withdrawn in 2010. Nevertheless, the US Federal government has been slow to examine alternative sites, or to resolve and fund research into alternatives, even though debate on nuclear fuel recycling is growing (CVP). An example of state-led action in the nuclear energy sector on the nuclear waste issue has occurred with the development of storage of low-level radioactive waste in Andrews County in Texas. This facility was given permission in April 2012, and may accept low-level nuclear waste from up to thirty-six states (Plushnick-Masti 2011; Schecter 2011).

The nuclear waste issue also suffers from being a 'wicked problem' – this is a type of problem which has a circular property where the question is shaped by the solution (Conklin 2003 in Nuttall 2005). Nuttall (2005) draws the connection between a wicked problem and radioactive waste management when considering the UK nuclear energy sector. According to Nuttall (2005), a wicked problem means that:

As each solution is proposed it exposes new aspects of the problem. Wicked problems are not amenable to the conventional linear approaches to solving complex problems. Such linear approaches go from gathering the necessary data, through analysing the data and formulating a solution towards implementation of a final agreed solution. By contrast, wicked problems can at one moment seem to be on the verge of solution, yet the next moment the problem has to be taken back to its complete fundamentals for further progress to be made. As such any opinion that the problem is almost solved is no indication that it actually is. Wicked problems can persist for decades and, for a true wicked problem, no solution will ever be possible. Wicked problems typically combine technical factors and social factors in complex multi-attribute trade-offs. A problem that is not wicked is said to be 'tame'. One thing is certain:

in the UK, at least, radioactive waste management is not a tame problem. (2005: 81)

It is evident that the nuclear waste issue in the US also features these 'wicked problem' characteristics. The Blue Ribbon Commission (BRC) has been given the task of suggesting solutions to the nuclear waste issue in the US, and in 2011 it stated that one of the primary motivations for solving the nuclear waste issue is to restore Federal-state relations which have deteriorated over the twenty years of court battles and indecision (Blue Ribbon Commission 2011). Indeed, its report (which does not suggest alternative sites to Yucca Mountain) acknowledges that public administration of the issue needs to be rectified, and in that context it states that a new organisation, independent of the Department of Energy (DOE), needs to be established (BRC 2011). This latter organisation will have full responsibility for the US nuclear waste programme. Further, the report recommended that the Nuclear Waste Fund ($750 million per year) needed to be set aside in the Federal budget and treated separately so that it can be used for its intended purpose (BRC 2011).

There are some positives occurring at the Federal level that may benefit nuclear energy and that are surmounting the policy inaction there. Laws drafted at other Federal level institutions can have an effect on the nuclear industry (H-2). This was not a consideration for many of those interviewed, but it was accepted as possible (CVP). Further, in light of the unwillingness of the Senate to vote on legislation creating a carbon market or a carbon tax it may happen to an increasing extent that laws drafted at other Federal institutions have an effect on the nuclear industry (4A, 4C, 4E). Already, the US EPA is trying to regulate the polluting effects from the oil, gas and coal industries via the Clean Air Act. The EPA asserts that it is protecting public health and the environment in targeting greenhouse gas emitting power plants – and it has power to do so through a 2007 Supreme Court ruling, *Massachusetts* v. *Environmental Protection Agency*, 549 U. S. 497 (2007). There is opposition to the EPA in this regard, arguing that EPA action will increase electricity prices, but the mere fact that this is happening demonstrates the potential of legislation created by other Federal institutions (beyond the DOE or NRC) to have an effect on the nuclear energy sector.

6.3.2   Hypothesis 2: Nuclear energy is an example of the failure to deliver large construction projects in the US on time and on budget

There are contrasting views surrounding this contested hypothesis. There is a belief among some interviewees that there exists the capability to build nuclear projects on time. However, other interviewees argue that they cannot. One interviewee (2B) summarises the issue by saying that in such a big project there will always be surprises:

> I think there will be challenges on any big construction project and nuclear is a big one so I think there will be some challenges that they're gonna have to overcome . . . so I think on a project like Vogtle 3 and 4 (Georgia) as they get into some detail there will be some surprises.

This hypothesis, although a contested hypothesis, was proven with the majority of interviewees were in favour of its acceptance. The principal reason for its acceptance, and the perspective advanced in this research, is that there has been a failure to understand the role of project management in the nuclear industry.

According to the majority of interviewees, new nuclear build is one of the most complex construction projects and has proved difficult to deliver on time and on budget in the past (CVP). Project management was poor in the US during the last nuclear build phase, and remains so (FNI-8). In the last period of nuclear new build, the projects were dominated by the classic problems cited in literature that lead to the failure of projects to deliver on time and on budget (see Table 6.4). Further, conditions have not improved yet in the US to deliver a nuclear new build project on time and on budget (4B). These problems identified by Flyvbjerg (2011) are not unique to the nuclear sector; however, nuclear energy projects seem to feature the majority of them. Indeed, Flyvbjerg (2011) states that the majority of (nearly nine out of ten) major projects are not built on time or on budget.

There are arguments that other countries can build nuclear power projects on time. However, there are three central reasons why other countries have built new reactors on time: (1) these projects were not the latest in nuclear technology – in countries where Generation III nuclear technology is being built, for example in France and Finland, there are major budgeted cost over-runs of €2.7 billion at the Finnish

Table 6.4 Reasons for failure in project management

Characteristics of projects that have failed to deliver on time or on budget

- Complex projects with long planning horizons
- Decision-making, planning, and management are typically multi-actor processes with conflicting interests
- Technology and designs are non-standard
- Project scope changes over time
- Over-commitment to a certain project concept
- Due to large sums of money involved, principal-agent problems are common
- Complexity and unplanned events are often unaccounted for, leaving budget and time contingencies sorely inadequate
- As a result of the latter, misinformation about costs, schedules, benefits and risks is the norm throughout project development and decision-making
- And therefore there are cost overruns and benefit shortfalls that undermine project viability during project implementation

Source: Compiled by the author from Flyvbjerg (2011: 322), 'Managing major projects'

Olkiluto reactor, and €1 billion at the French Flamanville reactor (De Beaupuy 2010); (2) working conditions in the US are not similar to those in China and South Korea; and (3) the companies building nuclear power in China and South Korea are government-owned and can thus obtain lower rates of interest for finance.

Proponents of the hypothesis state that little has changed since the last period when nuclear new build projects began construction (CVP), and this does not augur well for new projects. For example, public administration has not improved in terms of delivering a coherent long-term energy policy (CVP). Decision-making processes in the nuclear sector that involve multi-level actor groups are still not made according to a unified approach. For example, nuclear energy is cited as being one of the solutions in the battle against climate change, and also for US energy security and US energy independence, yet this is not supported at an administrative level to date. The Energy Policy Act of 2005, which incentivised nuclear new build and was responsible for eighteen applications for nuclear new build projects, has been slow in its implementation, as stated earlier. A major constant in the system remains, that mechanisms to deliver on policy in the form of outcomes are a weakness of the US public administration system (CVP).

The NRC, having been viewed as a contributor to the time delays and cost overruns in the last nuclear new built projects, has aimed to standardise the design process for new projects (CVP). As one interviewee (2D) stated: 'Cost overruns were just enormous and the Nuclear Regulatory Commission and the Department of Energy, they would have one formula to do criteria that you needed to meet and you'd meet it, and they'd change their mind and you had to go in and tear it out and start over again. Real expensive'. However, since then it has implemented a new licensing process in order to reduce the length of time it takes to go through the process and in order to provide more certainty in the process to potential operators. However, no company has tested the regime, and the Southern Nuclear project in Georgia will be the first to do so, hence delays can be expected there. These delays should not deter the nuclear industry as a whole as the new legal processes of the NRC will need to be modified, and these modifications will only benefit future applicants (CVP).

Conditions have not improved yet in the US for the delivery of a nuclear new build project on time and on budget (4B). Prospective nuclear new build projects face too much uncertainty in attempting to deliver on time and on budget (CVP). This problem will have to be rectified to increase the number of projects in the immediate future and requires more action in unison by actors in the nuclear sector (CVP). Public administration at a Federal level needs to improve as in essence these government officials have the responsibility to ensure that uncertainty in the nuclear sector is reduced, not increased by their involvement (CVP). The example of the Georgia new nuclear project demonstrates that, despite the success so far in the management of the Southern Nuclear project, it has been accused of going over budget and of being non-transparent about the issue by the Southern Alliance for Clean Energy environmental group (5G). Hence, project management issues remain, but as Flyvbjerg (2011) has stated, it is imperative that complexity and unplanned events have been accounted for in the project time schedule and financial budget. For the nuclear industry in the US, the Georgia project will have a significant effect on future nuclear new build (CVP).

6.3.3   Hypothesis 3: The unattractive economics of nuclear energy are the major reason the US nuclear industry has slowed down

There are contrasting viewpoints on why the nuclear renaissance has not occurred in the US. The unattractive economics of nuclear energy were cited by many of the interviewees as the main reason for the stalled state of nuclear new build projects in the US. However, the evidence points away from the economics of nuclear energy as the main reason why the nuclear renaissance has not happened in the US, and therefore this hypothesis is unproven, with a slim majority of the interviewees being critics of the hypothesis. In essence, economics are not the majority issue but just one reason among many for why the nuclear industry in the US has slowed down.

The economics of nuclear energy have made nuclear new build unattractive; however, there is a variety of other important reasons as to why new nuclear projects have stalled. In particular, these centre on the misconception of what the nuclear renaissance is, and the lack of improvements made to the public administrative system regarding nuclear energy in the US. Indeed, these issues result in uncertainty surrounding the continued growth of the nuclear sector. This uncertainty in the nuclear sector deters new investment, thus itself being a significant cause of the unattractive economics of such projects.

Understanding what a 'nuclear renaissance' is
There was a misconception among many experts and industry members as to what form a nuclear renaissance would take (4A). Nuttall (2005) also highlights that the term is only relevant for North America and Europe and not Asia, where expansion has progressed continuously. When the nuclear renaissance as a term first featured is stated by Nuttall (2005: 1–2), and Nuttall and Taylor (2009: 186–7) have discussed what the 'nuclear renaissance' means:

> Incidentally 'nuclear renaissance' is a phrase first coined in 1990 by Charles Venyvesi writing in *US News and World Report*. However the

phrase really started to take hold after it was used by Mark Yost in the *Wall Street Journal* on 13 September 1999 when he wrote: 'Not long ago, nuclear energy looked headed for extinction. Those days are over. With production costs dropping and regulations for fossil-fuel-burning plants rising, there's a renaissance taking place in nuclear power that would have been unthinkable five years ago.' We suggest that the seeds of renaissance were indeed sown at the turn of the millennium and now as we approach the end of the first decade of that millennium the renaissance is truly taking shape.

However, they do not offer or define what the nuclear renaissance would involve in terms of industry growth, and rate of expansion is mentioned by only a few authors (Goodfellow et al. 2011; Grimes and Nuttall 2010; Bradford 2009). The term 'nuclear renaissance' seems to have led to great expectations; however, it does not detail the expected or possible paths of evolution for the industry (4A, 4B). Numerous other sources of literature have stated that the industry would never again see the wave of expansion that occurred from the 1960s to the 1970s (Joskow and Baughman 1976; Rossin and Rieck 1978; Kasperson et al. 1980). Future phases of nuclear new build projects, they stated, would happen incrementally. It was the massive expansion in the 1960s and 1970s that resulted in the 104 operating reactors of today. However, it has also in part contributed to the slowdown in nuclear new build that has been experienced. The amount of power uprates and licensing renewals (see Table 6.2) that have occurred within the industry have negated some of the need for further nuclear new build (2B). However, while the nuclear renaissance has not happened to the degree that there are nuclear new build projects happening all across the country, there are some projects taking place (2B, 2C, 3B, 5B). The nuclear new build projects in Georgia and in South Carolina have begun construction, and there are several other plans ongoing to finish old previously near-complete reactors in other states, for example in Alabama by the Tennessee Valley Authority (Bellefonte Unit 2 which, from a previous construction phase, is already 55 per cent complete). In conclusion, the nuclear renaissance had not occurred by 2013, nor is it likely to occur. The full effect of Fukushima on nuclear new build will therefore be limited, as the industry had slowed already.

Lack of public administration improvement at Federal level

Nuclear energy has also suffered owing to a lack of improvements made to the public administrative system at a Federal level in the nuclear sector. As one interviewee (4E) stated: 'I think the big hurdles for nuclear are all technology and capital risk subsidies that . . . have to come from the Federal government . . . and you have to get a NRC permit and that is a pain in the neck and takes a long time . . . so it is mostly a Federal issue for nuclear'. Nuclear power has received no support from the US government through climate change and environmental incentive mechanisms. The Energy Policy Act of 2005 supported nuclear energy development through incentives, but Federal institutions have been slow to deliver these, as demonstrated earlier. There is no united action among Federal institutions, and indeed some interviewees pointed towards too much bureaucracy and the failure of public administration in the US (2B, 4A, 4B). Critics of the hypothesis – that the unattractive economics of nuclear energy are the major reason the US nuclear industry has slowed down – also stated that the current political tensions between Republicans and Democrats in the Senate mean that no Federal institutions want to implement new policies or changes (CVC). Further, inaction on a carbon market or carbon tax has failed to give nuclear energy a cost advantage regarding its non-CO_2-producing electricity production. The status quo of favouring the oil, gas and coal industries remains, for fear of hurting the US economy (CVC).

It is difficult, however, for the Federal institutions to operate as there is a question surrounding state rights. Where there are no rights or legislation explicitly given to the Federal system, the issue in question will fall under the jurisdiction of the state (i.e. because of the supremacy clause Article VI Clause 2 of the US Constitution). This has been documented in the literature and in particular in relation to the energy sector. Timney (2002) highlighted the problem in the electricity sector, where a lack of Federal regulation let speculators cause the California energy crisis. As a result, states had to become more proactive in the management of their energy sector or be susceptible to the lack of Federal governance (Timney 2002). Further, Kincaid and Cole (2005) in a public survey on state and US Federal issues asserted that there will be public support for national initiatives but enthusiasm for Federal programmes quickly recedes – they demonstrated this by using the 2011 terrorist attacks as an example. Hence, some critics of the hypothesis argued that too much expectation by industry is placed at a Federal level for implementing new policy (CVC). They state, similarly to Lutz (1992), that the Federal system in the US will guarantee a floor of rights and that development in rights for the individual will arise where states enter into competition with each other. If a similar scenario is said to be in existence in the US, it places more responsibility on the state rather than the Federal system in relation to finding a solution. Indeed, an individual state should be the innovator regarding new policy and legislation. However, there is an ongoing sway of power between the state and the Federal system aided by the pre-emptive statute where state and local feedback is sought prior to final amendment of statutes (Zimmerman 1990; Kincaid 1990).

The majority of energy policies emanating from Federal institutions that are implemented are short-term in nature so as to have a limited effect on electricity prices (4A, 4E, 4F, 5B). However, electricity policy does suffer from fragmentation, with each state having significant control over its own electricity policy – except for those in regional electricity markets, for example PJM. It is rather difficult, therefore, at a Federal level to have an impact upon state policy, as there will most likely be significant opposition from politicians to any Federal policies that will push up energy prices in their state. Hence, most action at Federal level is taken in the form of financial incentives or environmental and safety legislation, but all of this has been limited, as has been stated earlier. Any action on these issues that does transpire tends to be reduced in remit by the powerful lobby groups, of which the nuclear lobby is not one; hence action at a Federal level that results in positive outcomes for nuclear is rare (4A, 5B). For example, the 2005 Act stated that energy security (energy independence) was a key goal in US energy policy and nuclear was to assist in achieving these goals. However, support for this policy has not materialised to any significant degree at Federal level, and the nuclear industry has been left to the private sector with a slow implementation process for any of the incentive schemes established in the 2005 Act.

It follows from the above that nuclear energy issues are underrepresented at the Federal level. During the wave of nuclear expansion in the 1960s and 1970s, the development of a national nuclear lobby group received little attention. As a result, national lobby groups, lobby formations and networks do not as readily exist or are at an earlier stage of development than lobby groups, networks and associations for other energy sources – the Nuclear Energy Institute was only established in 1994. The NRC has the most significant role in the US nuclear energy sector. The Department of Energy also still plays a role with the Office of Nuclear Energy at the forefront; however, notably the Blue Ribbon Commission (2011) has suggested the establishment of a new independent institution to deal with the long-term radioactive waste issue. The Blue Ribbon Commission was a new institution established in 2010 and consists of fifteen members who were given responsibility to produce a report on the backend of the nuclear fuel cycle in the US.

Linked intrinsically to this issue is the problem of education on and surrounding nuclear energy issues. As stated earlier, nuclear energy is a complex subject and topic and there are even many employees across energy and nuclear energy institutions, not to mention the public, who do not understand all or many of the issues involved (2B, 4A, 5B). There is a need to develop and maintain expertise in the area. President Obama is a particular public advocate of the need to maintain expertise in nuclear energy. He stated, 'So make no mistake: Whether it's nuclear energy, or solar or wind energy, if we fail to invest in the technologies of tomorrow, then we're going to be importing those technologies instead of exporting them. We will fall behind. Jobs will be produced overseas, instead of here in the United States of America. And that's not a future that I accept' (17 February 2010). In any country, the issue of employment is of significance, and the nuclear energy sector is an important employer with a highly educated workforce, and this should be maintained (CVC). The above problems concerning the need for expertise have long been recognised in nuclear law and risk literature (Breyer 1978; Kasperson et al. 1980; Yellin 1981; Nelkin 1995; Palfreman 2006), and more recently in the Blue Ribbon Commission (2011) report on the future of nuclear energy in the US.

6.4 Conclusion

This chapter has examined, from a policy perspective, Federal policy in the nuclear energy sector in the US from 1990 to 2010. Public misconceptions of public administration, and project management and legal structural issues that exist for the planning of large infrastructure in the US have been identified. It has also been shown that there are cases of Federal policy inaction and contradiction, and that consequently state policy can be a key driver in encouraging the growth and operation of the nuclear industry.

First, the strength of Federal laws covering the nuclear energy sector was assessed. In general, it was determined there was policy inaction towards nuclear power at Federal level. An example of this inaction is evident in the weak application of the law such as the Energy Policy Act of 2005 which had a remit to re-ignite the industry, but has so far failed to have a significant influence on, or even to be applied to a significant degree to, nuclear energy. In addition to this, while the regulatory body for the sector, the Nuclear Regulatory Commission (NRC) has improved as an institution, it has achieved this improvement from a very low base. Consequently, there is an example of one state (Georgia) intervening in the sector and introducing its own law to provide more certainty to the nuclear sector by the introduction of Bill 31, which enacted the Georgia Nuclear Energy Financing Act in 2009. This permits the state utility, Georgia Power, to recover costs of construction from the beginning of the construction phase – these are known as Construction Work In Progress (CWIP) payments. Further, many of those interviewed expressed surprise about the progress of the project and that the project was near to being awarded the combined licence (COL) despite the inaction at Federal level concerning nuclear power.

Second, in the last period of nuclear new build, the projects were dominated by the failure to deliver on time and on budget. In the US, there remains a misunderstanding of the issue of project management for complex construction projects, and it is highly arguable whether many of these issues have been resolved. There remains some level of discord between many of the actor groups in the nuclear energy sector, as evidenced by delays in the regulatory process, and actions being taken by environmental groups. Yet it should be noted that the nuclear project in Georgia will be a test case for the regulatory process of the NRC and for many other factors in how to bring a nuclear project into operation in the US.

The final key issue discussed concerns the view that the economics of nuclear power form the major reason for nuclear new build being unattractive. The majority of those interviewed for this research opposed this latter view that economics of nuclear energy are the main reason and argued that there is a variety of other important reasons as to why new nuclear projects have stalled. In particular, these centre on the misconception of what the nuclear renaissance is, and the lack of improvement made to the public administrative system regarding nuclear energy in the US. Indeed, the problems due to the latter issues have resulted in major uncertainty surrounding the continued growth of the nuclear sector. This uncertainty in the nuclear sector deters new investment. However, the planned nuclear power project in Georgia demonstrates that a nuclear project can happen despite the negative attitudes that can emanate from the economics of nuclear power. President Obama's initial positive statements concerning growth in the nuclear sector have been rebuffed and negated. Public administrators have a role to play in the electricity sector and, as the Georgia case demonstrates, state-level action where there is widespread Federal policy inaction can be highly effective.

CHAPTER 7

Revising Energy Law and Policy in the UK: Re-igniting the Nuclear Energy Sector

7.1 Introduction

This chapter focuses on planned nuclear new build in the United Kingdom. The UK is embarking on an ambitious nuclear energy programme, the largest planned in Europe, and as such its nuclear energy policy may hold vital lessons for other countries intending to begin a new or similar nuclear power programme. Energy policy regarding nuclear energy has fluctuated over the last decade; however, it has now been given a strong mandate by government. In order to achieve a sustainable nuclear energy policy, three issues are of major importance: (1) law, policy and development; (2) public administration; and (3) project management. The focus on these three issues builds on the analysis from the earlier chapters and with more clarity energy law and policy can be deconstructed. The analysis in the chapter identifies that policy issues remain to be resolved in the energy sector, in particular at an institutional and legal level. However, contrary to the literature, in some areas a change of course is being witnessed as the UK concentrates on delivering a long-term policy for the nuclear energy sector and the overall energy sector.

7.2 Background to the UK electricity sector

The UK electricity industry is about to undergo a major transformation. It is set for major investment, with a government White Paper in 2011 on electricity (entitled Planning Our Electric Future, hereafter referred to as the '2011 White Paper') suggesting that a £110 billion investment is required by 2020. This is more than double the planned rate of investment (as of 2012). The 2011 White Paper also states that within the next decade a quarter (around 20GW) of existing generation capacity will be lost and this will need to be replaced to avoid any potential '*costly blackouts*' (Department of Energy and Climate Change 2011a: 5, italics added). Yet there is a limited amount of research that focuses on new electricity generation in the UK. With literature on electricity and nuclear energy policy being interdisciplinary, this research does not aim to cover the problems encountered across the full range of academic disciplines, but instead focuses on the management and delivery of new generation and in particular nuclear energy, which is viewed as one of the solutions to the UK problem outlined above.

The government has expressed concern surrounding the 20GW of new electricity generation capacity that is needed over the next decade. In taking into account the long planning permission processes of the UK, and the construction times for major new investment, there needs to be some significant development soon. The 2011 White Paper specifically mentions nuclear energy as an option, yet the last nuclear plant in the UK took seven years to build, and this on top of a six-year planning and review process – hence it took thirteen years to bring into operation from the date of the first application for a site and design licence (British Energy 2011; Department for Business Enterprise and Regulatory Reform 2006). This time period is too long for the government's policy needs.

The question arises: can the current institutional arrangements efficiently spend and deliver on this £110 billion investment in the electricity sector? This research examines the UK electricity sector in the context of nuclear new build. The focus of the research question revolves around the term 'delivery' and delivery of the planned nuclear power programme. With the UK facing many years of austerity budgeting, the importance of delivering on the investment of £110 billion in the electricity sector has to be stressed.

Nuclear energy contributes around 18 per cent of the UK's electricity through the operation of seventeen reactors (see Table 7.1) – the figure was only 16 per cent in 2010 due to maintenance outages but was 18 per cent in 2009. However, the problem for the UK is the expected closure of sixteen of these nuclear power reactors, all by 2023.

As shown in Table 7.2, three reactor designs are present in the UK market: fourteen of the reactors in the UK are advanced gas cooled reactors (AGRs), two Magnox reactors, and one pressurised water

Table 7.1 Shares of net electricity supplied in the UK in 2010

Supply source	Share of electricity supplied by source (%)
Gas	47%
Coal	28%
Nuclear	16%
Renewable energy	7%
Other fuels	1%
Imports	1%

Source: Compiled by the author from Department of Energy and Climate Change (2011b), Digest of United Kingdom Energy Statistics 2011

Table 7.2 Nuclear reactors in operation in the UK in 2012

Location	Reactor design	Number of reactors	Capacity (MW)	Unextended lifetime
Wyfla	Magnox	2	980	1971–2012
Hinkley Point B	AGR	2	1220	1976–2016
Hunterston B	AGR	2	1190	1976–2016
Dungeness B	AGR	2	1110	1985–2018
Heysham	AGR	2	1160	1989–2019
Hartlepool	AGR	2	1190	1989–2019
Heysham 2	AGR	2	1250	1989–2023
Torness	AGR	2	1250	1988–2023
Sizewell B	PWR	1	1188	1995–2035
Total		17	10755	

Source: Compiled by the author from Department of Energy and Climate Change (2013)

Table 7.3 Nuclear new build plans in the UK

Company	Locations	Number, type and capacity of reactors	First nuclear concrete*
1. NNB GenCo	Hinkley Sizewell	2 x 1600 MW EPRS 2 x 1600 MW EPRS	Expected 2016
2. Horizon Nuclear Power Ltd	Wylfa Oldbury	3GW at each site, technology choice undecided	Expected: unknown
3. Nu-Generation	Moorside (Sellafield)	3GW at the site, technology choice undecided	Expected: unknown

*First nuclear concrete – the date construction is expected to begin.
Source: Department of Energy and Climate Change (2011c; 2013) and Nuclear Industry Association (2011)

reactor (PWR). It is expected that the AGRs will receive a lifetime extension of five to seven years while the PWR operators are planning for a twenty-year lifetime extension (NEI 2012).

With these closures expected (even despite the small lifetime extension), the UK has developed a new nuclear programme that envisages ten reactors being built on five sites in the UK by three different companies. This is outlined in Table 7.3. It is evident from this table that NNB GenCo is further advanced and expected its first nuclear plant of the nuclear new build programme to become operational in 2018 (Department of Energy and Climate Change 2011a); however, this is unlikely to be the case. Further, neither of the other two companies (Horizon and NuGen) has yet fully confirmed its reactor design, and overall their projects are some way off in terms of timing when compared with the NNB GenCo project. Horizon, in particular, suffered a major setback when in March 2012 RWE and EoN announced they were withdrawing from the company and sold it to Hitachi. There was also further concern over NNB GenCo with Centrica withdrawing from its investment in the nuclear new build in the UK.

Statements in the analysis that follows are supported by the critics or proponents of the hypothesis and in these cases the reference code is CVP (Consensus View of Proponents), and CVC (Consensus View of the Critics). In the analysis that follows, specific quotes or opinions gathered from the interview process are referenced with an interview code that corresponds to those listed in the Appendix, with a number corresponding to the interviewee's category of institution, and a letter to his or her specific institution.

7.3   Renewing energy law and policy in the UK: uncontested issues

It was accepted by the majority of the interviewees that energy policy in the UK has suffered from a short-term perspective. This perspective was prevalent and permeated across the legal, economic and the public administration systems in the UK. Indeed, it was this short-term influence on policy that contributed to uncertainty in the energy sector and resulted in a lack of investment in new generation, and this is particularly evident in the nuclear energy sector. Successive UK governments have developed policy over the period since the 2008 White Paper on Nuclear Power (and even before that) which set out to provide assurances to the private sector that the sector is ready for investment. This coincided with the recognition that change was required to encourage investment and that a long-term strategy regarding nuclear energy policy was needed.

As will be discussed in more detail later, the electricity market needed to be re-designed. The liberalisation of the UK electricity sector had worked in some respects but not in others. Its goal of increasing efficiency of operation within the sector has been achieved: however, this has come at a cost: namely, a lack of investment in new electricity generation infrastructure. Further, since the market was liberalised, the objectives of the electricity market have changed. Climate change and energy security have become major policy drivers for the UK government over the past ten years, and the liberalised electricity market was not really designed to meet these aims. As a consequence, the government has set about reforming the electricity market to ensure that new generation capacity is built in the UK and that it is from low-carbon sources. Energy security and climate change targets are long-term policies by nature and this has created the need to reorient energy economics so as to achieve long-term economic aims.

Legal and policy revisionism have occurred over the past decade in the UK in relation to the energy sector, but this was an expected consequence of short-term policy aims. Nevertheless, the industry has had other concerns. Nuclear new build projects have a history of being over budget and over time. However, the majority of interviewees stated that this is a characteristic of many major infrastructure and big-budget projects, and therefore nuclear energy projects are not unique. Further, nuclear new build projects do not receive more publicity in this regard. Rather, the majority of large infrastructure projects have this characteristic of being over budget and over time and therefore receive publicity to this effect. For example, currently in the UK, offshore wind projects and the 2012 Olympics both received high levels of publicity about their potential to deliver on time and on budget.

Another concern for a new nuclear power programme in the UK has been the lack of human resources in the sector. The last nuclear project in the UK was at Sizewell B, which was completed in 1995. The vast majority of staff employed on that build project have now retired. However, while the education of the next generation of staff for the nuclear energy sector is of importance to the sector, it is not a weakness in the sector. When investment decisions are finally made on the next nuclear projects in the UK, then it is expected that companies will allocate resources to the nuclear sector. The government and universities have been proactive in this regard, but further investment in the area will need the nuclear programme to have a confirmed beginning.

The final hypothesis concerned the effect of Fukushima on the nuclear energy sector in the UK. All interviewees were in agreement that they were surprised at the minimal effect that Fukushima had had on the sector thus far. The reasons for this were, according to the majority, that the UK has a good reputation for safety, and a good safety culture in the nuclear sector. The view was also expressed that it was important that there had not been an over-reaction to events in Japan. A minority of interviewees even expressed surprise that the only effect had been a possible six- to twelve-month delay to the developing nuclear energy programme, and this amidst an economic crisis and with one of the political parties (the Liberal Democrats) in government having been previously opposed to nuclear power.

7.4   Renewing energy law and policy in the UK: contested issues (hypotheses)

7.4.1   Hypothesis 1: Planning law difficulties are different for nuclear energy projects

For this hypothesis the consensus view of the critics (CVC) holds and the hypothesis is unproven, as the analysis that follows demonstrates. Contrasting views of the public sector and the private sector are evident, the latter more critical and the former having an equal percentage for and against the hypothesis. The planning process is under the operation of the public sector, so it could be expected that this stakeholder category would be against stating that nuclear energy suffered more difficulties in the planning process than other infrastructure projects.

However, within the interviews, recognition was given to the changes that have occurred in the planning process and that, while nuclear energy was a driver of that change – to fast-track major projects through the planning process – the experience of the nuclear industry with the planning process was not restricted to just their industry sector. A significant view raised in the literature is that nuclear energy development had a significant role in the development of the new planning system (Robinson 2009). This was because the government estimated that there is a need for nuclear new build in order to replace existing nuclear power plants (CVP) (expressed also in the National Policy Statement for Nuclear Power Generation (EN-6)). It states that nuclear energy, unlike other energy sources, faces longer planning consultation periods, though wind energy projects are also experiencing long planning consultation times. In comparison, in the 1990s forty-four applications to build combined cycle gas turbine installations consents were granted with few public inquiries (Select Committee on Trade and Industry 1998). Yet the reason as to why nuclear energy projects result in longer planning processes is not stated. This research aims to fill this gap in the literature. For more detailed analysis, see section 3.3.1 of this volume, but to reiterate, the literature that does exist points towards three recurrent themes:

1. While the planning system needed to be reformed to reduce the length of the process, this should not occur if the due process of

law is not upheld (Robinson 2009; Grekos 2010; Clarke and Cummins 2011).

2. Law in the area will have to be reviewed once other connecting policy goals are established (Commons Energy and Climate Change Committee 2011; Bircham, Dyson and Bell 2009).

3. Legislating for the unknown, and proactive legislation (Robinson 2009; Commons Energy and Climate Change Committee 2011).

Critics of the hypothesis (CVC) also point towards several other key issues that demonstrate nuclear energy projects face the same hurdles as other large infrastructure projects. In particular, wind energy projects are facing distinct local opposition, although this is different from the opposition that nuclear energy projects have faced in the past, which has tended to be from national environmental movements and not at local level (where they receive support in many cases, for example at Wylfa in Wales). Other major projects, such as coal plant projects, Heathrow Terminal 5 and the prospective high-speed rail project (HS2 – London to Birmingham high-speed rail project) would receive as much opposition, or more, in the planning process as a nuclear energy project (CVC). Already, the search for shale gas in the UK is receiving strong objections owing to the fracking process involved (CVC). However, one interviewee from the public sector category (5B) stated:

> Objections need not always be considered to be detrimental to the project in terms of contributing to delay. In some cases, they can benefit a project: Greenpeace contributions to the consultation processes for the 2008 White Paper on Nuclear Power actually identified areas of clarification and helped create a more complete published White Paper at the end of the process.

7.4.2   Hypothesis 2: Public administration in the nuclear energy sector is in need of change

This section of the research in essence examines the role of public administration in the electricity sector. In particular, it focuses on its role and effect on the nuclear energy sector. The issue revolves around whether the public administration system in the UK encourages or inhibits the development of new electricity generation in the UK. In this context, the hypothesis is directed at assessing whether the public institutions and organisations in the sector are adequate, in need of change, renewal, or replacement by new ones. Theory in the area advocates that change has been needed, as will be discussed later.

The hypothesis is a contested hypothesis, and overall a majority of interviewee respondents rejected it. Based on these responses and the analysis that follows, this hypothesis is also unproven. However, what must be noted in the context of this hypothesis is the amount of change in public administration that has occurred to date (detailed below). Consequently, interviewees were able to express the view that no longer was the public administration system in the energy and nuclear sectors in need of change. Yet the overall figure of 38 per cent who agreed with the hypothesis is a considerably high figure. The Academic Researcher category view is strongly in favour of the hypothesis and several individuals within this category identified the need for and location of further changes in the public administration system. With the policy and legislative process still uncompleted for the reform of the electricity market, there is perhaps merit to the argument of the proponents of this hypothesis. The analysis that follows assesses change in public administration in the nuclear energy sector from two perspectives, that of: (1) legislative and policy change; and (2) institutional change.

Legislative and policy change
The UK's current policy on energy infrastructure planning has over the past decade been undergoing a transition. Consistency has not been at the forefront of policy development. Table 7.4 outlines the major policy and legal development over the past decade. Yet the 2011 White Paper (listed in Table 7.4) still has to be resolved. This 2011 White Paper and the subsequent Energy Act 2013 centre on reforming the electricity market and, notably, Haye (2012) has stated that this reform is not likely to be finalised until 2014, and this is likely due to the need for EU approval.

The initial transition was greatly influenced by the 2002 Energy Review and, in turn, the 2003 White Paper Our Energy Future: Creating a Low Carbon Economy (Department of Trade and Industry 2003). The 2002 and 2003 documents represented a shift in attitudes about the UK's energy strategy, framed in terms of a response to commitments made by the UK government to reduce

Table 7.4 Policy and legal development in the electricity sector

White Papers and legislation, 2002–11

2002	The Energy Review
2002	Managing the Nuclear Legacy – A Strategy for Action
2003	Energy White Paper: Our Energy Future – Creating a Low Carbon Economy
2006	The Energy Challenge: Energy Review Report 2006
2007	Energy White Paper on Energy 2007. Meeting the Energy Challenge
2007	Planning for a Sustainable Future White Paper
2008	Meeting the Energy Challenge: A White Paper on Nuclear Power
2008	Energy Act chapter 32
2008	Climate Change Act chapter 27
2008	Planning Act chapter 29
2009	The UK Low Carbon Transition Plan: National Strategy for Climate and Energy
2009	The Road to 2010: Addressing the Nuclear Question in the Twenty First Century
2011	Planning Our Electric Future: A White Paper for Secure, Affordable and Low-carbon Electricity

carbon emissions, and to assess energy security. There was a particular reference to the need to build new energy infrastructure and this was to involve the construction of a large number of renewable energy projects around the country. Nuclear energy did not feature prominently in the 2003 White Paper, and according to some interviewees it was due to the Prime Minister's office which insisted on its inclusion that it received any mention. Of significance was that the option was kept open, and that it stated that the problem of nuclear waste needed to be addressed.

Several of the interviewees from the public sector category stated that it was at this point that the prospects for new nuclear energy projects began to be considered. Plans were made to begin a new nuclear programme; however, at first other issues within the sector needed to be resolved, in particular the waste issue (A-PS). Further, it was also necessary to keep nuclear energy off the main political agenda due to the performance of British Energy and the publicly funded bailout of this company (over 2002 to 2004, and as approved by the European Commission (Europa 2005).

In 2006 the UK Department of Trade and Industry produced another Energy Review, assessing the UK's progress towards the medium and long-term goals of the 2003 Energy White Paper. The 2006 review reinforced the need to build more large-scale renewable projects and represented a *public* shift in government attitudes towards nuclear energy, advocating an expansion of nuclear power, through Generation III nuclear power plants (CVC).

In the 2007 White Paper, Meeting the Energy Challenge, the UK government set out its energy strategy, based on 'tackling climate change' and 'ensuring secure, clean and affordable energy' (Department of Trade and Industry 2007: 6), a strategy that formed the basis of the 2008 Energy Act. The year 2008 was significant in that it also saw the creation of the Department of Energy and Climate Change (DECC) to lead energy policy development in the UK. A new department had been considered before, and Maugis and Nuttall (2008) had noted that this type of reform had been an issue since 2003. DECC was given a Cabinet seat and was formed from the Climate Change Group in the Department for Environment, Food and Rural Affairs (DEFRA) and the Energy Group from the Department for Business, Enterprise and Regulatory Reform (BERR). Also in 2008, three other government outputs were to modify the UK's approach to energy and energy infrastructure planning: the White Paper on Nuclear Power; the Planning Act; and the Climate Change Act, and the key implications of each output will be noted.

The White Paper on Nuclear Power, produced by the then Department for Business Enterprise and Regulatory Reform (2008), stated very clearly the modification to the UK government's energy strategy in relation to nuclear power:

> The Government believes it is in the public interest that new nuclear power stations should have a role to play in this country's future energy mix alongside other low-carbon sources; that it would be in the public interest to allow energy companies the option of investing in new nuclear power stations; and that the Government should take active steps to open up the way to the construction of new nuclear power stations. (2008: 10)

This was a formal indication that new nuclear power generation should be developed as part of the UK's energy mix beyond 2020 and provided an indication that new nuclear power stations would be planned and constructed with an emphasis on this plan being government-driven.

Coupled with these two policy statements came the UK's 2008 Climate Change Act. This reconfirmed the UK's commitment to carbon emission reduction, which under the Kyoto Protocol set a 12.5 per cent reduction of 1990 emission levels, and indeed extended and formalised the UK commitment to an 80 per cent reduction of carbon emissions on 1990 levels by 2050.

In 2010 UK government policy on energy provision reached a state of tension. One tension point was that the parties comprising the new UK coalition government had expressed different manifesto commitments on energy; a second was that, in Scotland and Wales, the devolved governments have each expressed the importance of developing large-scale renewable projects in their jurisdiction, along with each also having expressed opposition to new nuclear power stations (Scottish Government 2008). Indeed, Scotland has moved further on its own course than Wales, and in 2008 the Scottish Parliament produced its own energy policy document for Scotland.

The current literature is somewhat divided on the issue of the effect of Scottish devolution on UK energy policy. The Scotland Act 1998 which created the new Scottish Parliament appears to have given Scotland extensive powers regarding the formulation of its own environmental policy (Little 2000). However, as Little (2000) determines, there are limiting factors such as the need to adhere to international and EU environmental law as well as the provisions for judicial review and political review by the UK government. In this context, Keating (2010) argues that while Scottish devolution may be limited by intergovernmental relations with both the UK and the EU in many policy areas, there are opportunities for policy innovation. Hence, while developing its own environmental policy may be a limited exercise, Scotland has the capability to pursue its own energy policy. It remains to be seen how far Scotland may diverge in its approach to its energy policy with that of the UK, and as yet the only distinctive difference with the rest of the UK has been the decision not to build new nuclear reactors. It is arguable therefore that energy policy has fragmented to a degree within the UK. Though this is a topic to consider in more depth in future, it can be stated that the Scottish move in 2008 to have its own energy policy has added to the uncertainty in the development of a long-term UK energy policy, in particular because of the 'no-nuclear new build' decision.

In 2011 a new White Paper, entitled Planning Our Electric Future, was presented by the Department of Energy and Climate Change, and the key elements of this White Paper were intended to become law by 2013 (Department of Energy and Climate Change 2011a: 13). This was the case and the Energy Act 2013 was passed. The White Paper itself was an attempt to develop a long-term energy policy in the UK, and alongside the Renewables Roadmap (2011), details proposals for a major expansion of large-scale projects by 2020. Many of the details that flowed from the 2011 White Paper were expected to take some time to be finalised (in particular, regarding the exact benefits given to new low-carbon infrastructure projects), this means that there remains potential for further change (CVP). Consequently, the next sub-section assesses the hypothesis from an institutional change perspective.

Institutional change
Policy at a national level in the UK in the energy sector has been in a transitional phase, as argued earlier and shown in Table 7.1. Since privatisation emerged as government policy, the electricity sector has been subject to constant tweaks and revisions. Whether the policy of privatisation has been a success is debatable with the lack of any real strategies for investing in the future of the electricity system. It was recognised by the government with Chris Huhne, the former Secretary of State for Energy and Climate Change, stating in his Foreword to the 2011 White Paper Planning Our Electric Future that 'since the market was privatised in the 1980s the system has worked: delivering secure and affordable electricity for the UK. But it cannot meet the challenges of the future' (2011: 3).

Yet this raises questions about the operation of the public sector in overseeing the privatised electricity sector. There was a clear lack of unity in what the objective of privatisation of the electricity sector ought to be. The evidence points to it having been a process to correct prices and improve operational efficiency (see earlier discussion of Hypothesis 9). It is arguable whether it has achieved anything else. Indeed, OFGEM (2011) produced a report highlighting collusion among the electricity market companies, which have also formed an oligopoly where six firms control and own 99 per cent of the supply market.

According to the majority of those interviewed, however, it is evident, that the Electricity White Paper 2011 has the clear ambition to introduce a long-term focus, and this represents an improvement on previous policies. This long-term focus is unique in British politics according to one interviewee (3A), who stated that:

> The government has currently published a paper on electricity market reform, which is precisely about the long-term. It's got a Climate Change Act to 2050. There's never before in the whole history in the UK been anything as long-sighted as that. Now they may not have thought it through properly [. . .] I don't think we've had in history anything that's the equivalent of the Climate Change Act. And it used to be thought that that sort of thing wouldn't be possible for political reasons. You know, governments are only elected for one term, so how can you set a legally binding target for 2050? [. . .] with all the small print about whether it's really effective, but still they've done it. And they've done it in a consensual cross-party way, with all three parties essentially agreeing with it, and it is long term, and it sets clear targets [. . .] The structure of policy-making (in this area) I think is remarkably long term.

This decision-making by the UK government marks a major change to theory in public administration. Prior development of energy policy in the UK was symptomatic of the management and organisation of public services across the world. Indeed, Ferlie et al. (2005) stated that public administration services were 'moving through an intriguing and even disorientating period across the world' (2005: 1). In terms of energy policy, and in particular electricity policy, it has emerged in the UK that over the past few decades the UK public service (administration) has lost some if its vital functions. The UK privatisation process in the electricity sector resulted in a transfer of control in the coordination and management of some activities. Some of these transfers were desired of course, but some were neither expected nor planned. The key function lost was the ability to add new generation capacity to the market in response to future demands or because of policy changes (such as carbon reduction). Thus, the government has set out to rectify this problem concerning the provision of new generation through its recent White Paper Planning Our Electric Future, with the government intending to take a lead role in the management of the development of the sector. Taylor (1911, 1916), who coined the phrase 'scientific management', saw the role of public services as being to monitor and incentivise, and had the public sector in the UK completed these functions the current requirement for massive investment in the electricity sector might not have been necessary.

Lynn (2005: 45) has advocated the reasoning of several other academics in assessing any modern public administration system:

1. Jann (1997: 4) stated that '[a]ll administrative reform, like all administrative theory, deals with the same set of problems: legality, [. . .] legitimacy, [. . .] efficiency and effectiveness' (1997: 94).
2. Raadschelders and Rutgers (1999: 30) argued that 'public administration cannot be understood at all' without studying the three dichotomies – public/private, policy/administration, and state/society.
3. Aucoin and Neintzman (2000: 46) claimed that '[a]ll governments, must now govern in a context where there are greater demands for accountability for performance on the part of a better educated and less deferential citizenry, more assertive and well organised interest groups and social movements, and more aggressive and intrusive mass media operating in a highly competitive information-seeking and processing environment'.

Understanding these three views represents the direction that the public administration has taken to some degree in the nuclear energy sector. Nevertheless, the need for further action still remains. Indeed, interviewees from the public sector category (A-PS) stated that the reorganisation of the nuclear sector was necessary to deliver legitimacy and effectiveness to the sector, as well as to have a system that was accountable and proactive in this regard. Further, the role of public administration is not to be seen in isolation: the new nuclear energy institutions have in their remit the requirement to work and develop relationships with the private sector and the public (A-PS).

Table 7.5 New public administration institutions established in the nuclear energy sector since 2002

Institution	Established
Nuclear Decommissioning Authority	2004
The National Skills Academy – Nuclear	2007
Department of Energy and Climate Change	2008
Office of Nuclear Development	2009
Nuclear Liabilities Financing Assurance Board	2009
Office for Nuclear Regulation	2011

The critics of this hypothesis point towards the public administration system in the UK having gone through change to reorient itself from having a short-term to long-term perspective and hence no more being needed (CVC). The list of institutions formed over the last decade is recorded in Table 7.5, which demonstrates the change that was needed.

This section of the research has examined the role of public administration in the electricity sector. There has been significant development of law, policy and institutional structures. Time is needed to embed these new policies and structures; however, a minority of those interviewed still believe that further change is needed. In essence, they question whether the new structures represent the new long-term perspective and commitment needed for the energy sector and if they have addressed how to be effective in the delivery of the nuclear energy programme.

7.4.3   Hypothesis 3: 'Project management' is a misunderstood term in the nuclear energy sector

For the beginning is thought to be more than half the whole (Aristotle, *Ethics*: Book 1.C.4)

This section concentrates on how the practice of project management is understood in relation to nuclear new build projects. A major concern of nuclear new build projects has to do with whether they will be built on time and on budget (Taylor 2011). Project management as a research field has developed significantly since its emergence in the 1950s and is now regarded as a sub-discipline of management research (Morris et al. 2011). While there is a focus on 'megaprojects' in the literature, there remains a dearth of literature that is nuclear-specific. Considering the scale and cost of nuclear new build projects and their history of non-completion on time or on budget, there is a gap in the literature which this research seeks to fill. Similarly, Flyvbjerg and COWI (2004) and Wachs (1986, 1990), in completing their work on project management, have carried out interviews with those in the sector such as managers, public officials, planners and consultants.

Overall, a strong majority of respondents agreed with the hypothesis and this was the case across nearly all categories of interviewees. Notably, the private sector had the highest percentage of interviewees who were against the hypothesis. This is relevant to the discussion that follows in relation to optimism bias and strategic misrepresentation regarding time and budgets on nuclear energy projects. As a result of the analysis that follows, and coupled with the interview analysis, this hypothesis was proven.

Nuclear new build projects exhibit all the classic signs of failure in project management, which have been listed by Flyvbjerg (2011) (see Table 6.4 in the previous chapter). Indeed, the majority of interviewees stated that many of these characteristics listed were problems that have arisen in the nuclear projects in Flamanville in France and Olkiluoto in Finland (CVP). In their view these problems provide lessons to be learnt for the planned nuclear projects in the UK (CVP).

The UK has outlined its plans to have a new nuclear energy programme with the potential for up to ten reactors at five different sites (the number depends on what reactor is chosen by Horizon and NuGen; see Table 7.3). Taylor (2007, 2011) outlines in his analysis of the nuclear industry in the UK that project cost over-runs were a feature of the last phase of nuclear new build in the UK. In these times of austerity, therefore, completing nuclear projects on time and on budget is of particular importance for the future development of the industry and, hence, underlines the importance of research into project management.

At first instance, project management is associated with completing a project on time and on budget. However, project management concerns more than completing a project efficiently on time, on budget and to specification. The management of projects is an organisational entity in its own right and covers 'their context and front-end development and definition as well as their realization; and [is] concerned with doing this effectively so that value is built and benefit realization is optimised' (Morris et al. 2011: 4). Project management seeks to add value and has a long-term orientation. For a nuclear new build project, the actual point when the project management phase begins is at the very beginning when the decision is being contemplated as to whether to build or not, which arguably begins at government level. However, only a small minority of those interviewed recognised that this needed to be the case. From this minority, who were in the public sector category (A-PS), the interviewees stated that this same view from the literature – that project management begins at the policy formulation stage – had only in recent years begun to be applied in the nuclear energy sector.

The literature identifies projects according to different categorisations, as outlined in Table 7.6. Nuclear new build fits across several of these project types and typologies, and this demonstrates the need for its assessment in project management terms. This list is not complete, but it serves as an indication of the types of projects, and the possibilities for learning from other projects.

There is much to learn for nuclear energy projects from the success and failures of other major projects, for example: Heathrow Terminal 5; the Eurotunnel; and the 2012 Olympics (CVP). Nuclear new build projects are not unique in having a history of running over budget and over time. The majority of interviewees stated that this is a characteristic of many major infrastructure and big-budget projects (H7). Indeed, Flyvbjerg (2011) stated that nine out of ten projects have cost overruns with these overruns as high as 50 per cent to 100 per cent. Flyvbjerg et al. (2009) suggested that the root cause of underperformance is that project planners tend systematically to underestimate or even ignore risks of complexity, scope changes, and so on during project development and decision-making. At the most basic level, Flyvbjerg et al. (2009) identified and grouped into three

Table 7.6   Project types and typologies

	Types/typologies
Size	Major projects Large engineering projects Mega-projects Grand-scale projects
Institutional and industry context	Public projects Industry type projects
Organisational condition	Global projects Inter-organisational projects Cross-functional projects Embedded projects

Task features	Business development and change projects
	Complexity, uncertainty (technological, novelty), pace
	CoPS projects (Complex Products and Systems)
	Uncertainty (variation, foreseen uncertainty,
	    unforeseen uncertainty, chaos
	Renewal projects
	Exploration and exploitation projects
	    (vanguard projects)
	Repetitive and unique projects
	Derivative, platform, breakthrough

Source: Compiled by the author from Soderlund (2011: 44)

categories the causes of project underperformance (adapted from Flyvbjerg 2011: 323–9):

1. *Bad luck or error*: this has been refuted as Flyvbjerg (2011) asserts that it should always be factored in, and the answer lies in the other two categories.
2. *Optimism bias* (psychological): managers fall victim to the planning fallacy where they base decisions on delusional optimism rather than on rational weighting of gains, losses and probabilities.
3. *Strategic misrepresentation* (political) accounts for flawed planning and decision-making in terms of political pressures and agency issues. Politicians, planners and/or project promoters deliberately or

strategically underestimate the time and/or costs of the project in order that their project gains approval or funding.

The majority of interviewees were in agreement that optimism bias and/or strategic misrepresentation were prevalent in the costing of nuclear energy projects (CVP). This issue of costing had a negative effect on the nuclear industry (CVP). However, it was recognised that this was not a unique problem for nuclear projects, but was a feature of many public and private projects. The literature puts forward a solution called 'reference class forecasting', based on the work of Daniel Kahneman (1994; 1979 with Tversky), which analysed bias and uncertainty in decision-making, and advanced by Flyvbjerg (2011). However, the application of this costing technique or the potential of other techniques has limited value in practice (CVP) because of the political and economic issues facing the public and private sector. Projects that cost too much from the outset will never happen; and because there are commercially sensitive issues and strategy at play, neither politicians nor CEOs want to endorse high-cost and risky projects (CVP). In 2005, however, reference class forecasting was endorsed by the American Planning Association (2005), and since then it has been used in many countries. It involves three steps: (1) identification of a relevant reference class of past projects; (2) establishing a probability distribution for the selected class; and (3) comparing the specific project with the reference class distribution (Flyvbjerg 2011: 331). However, this costing technique has not yet been employed by the nuclear industry. Critics of the hypothesis argue that project management techniques are well understood, but it is because these projects are the first of a kind in terms of technology that they are expensive. They cite the learning effect that will materialise should a programme of reactors be built and the standardisation of the design as key factors as to why this this nuclear power programme will mean nuclear projects can be built on time and to budget (CVC). Further, the majority of those interviewed, both critics and proponents of the hypothesis, stated that the industry needs to do more to learn from the nuclear new build projects in China and South Korea. And this search for knowledge should not be focused on the projects alone but on national energy policy, the nuclear supply chain and the actions of the regulators.

7.5   Conclusion

This chapter has focused on the period 2002–12 and how nuclear energy policy developed over that time in the UK. The research centres on the conditions for planned nuclear new build to occur in the UK. The conclusions reached after the research analysis are that three issues come to the fore: planning law, public administration, and project management.

The literature suggests that the planning process plays a distinctive role in delaying nuclear new build projects. However, the research points towards this not being unique to the nuclear sector, and that difficulties with the planning process in the UK are present for the majority of other large-scale infrastructure developments. Further, a previous Labour government had recognised this issue and changed the planning laws in order to fast-track large infrastructure projects through the planning system. In essence, this involved the determination of national issues through the use of NPSs, consequently leaving only local issues to be considered in planning inquiries. Whether this change in legislation will have the desired effect is open to question, as there is little or no practice under the new regime to date.

The second major point of analysis assessed the change in public administration in the nuclear energy sector from two perspectives: (1) legislative and policy change; and (2) institutional change. Literature in the area points towards public administration systems that are too short-term oriented and in need of structural reform. The major steps taken in the UK towards reform of the energy sector were demonstrated, in particular those concerning the nuclear energy sector. This has been an ongoing process over the last decade and arguably has another few years until it is finalised. The depth of the problem with the public administration system in the UK in the energy sector is highlighted through the wave of policy documents published by successive governments over the past decade. Further, the nuclear energy public administration sector has been transformed with the creation of six new public organisations in the area. Despite this change, 38 per cent of interviewees still believed that further reform is necessary. It is notable, however, that public institutions acknowledge that change had to occur for reasons similar to those suggested within the literature.

The final issue analysed in this chapter is project management and the misunderstanding of the concept among the stakeholders in the UK nuclear energy sector. The present research brings some degree of order to the disorder surrounding the concept. Project management, as the literature suggests, begins at the policy-formulation level when a new policy is being planned, and this approach has benefits for the entirety of the sector. In the UK, this approach has been applied in the nuclear energy sector to a degree. Another misunderstanding regarding project management is the delivery of projects on time and on budget. While it is acknowledged that projects may be complex and overrun for other unavoidable reasons, two key reasons present themselves: optimism bias and strategic misrepresentation. Nuclear projects are not unlike other projects in this regard and these two elements are present when time and cost projections for nuclear projects are being completed. Further, the literature states that the majority of large projects are over time and over budget. Hence, nuclear energy projects are not alone in this respect, but nevertheless the industry is not excluded from seeking solutions. In this context, the majority of those interviewed pointed towards the lessons that can be learned from nuclear projects in China and South Korea, and these studies would also incorporate assessments of the work culture, regulator performance, and the nuclear supply chain.

CHAPTER 8

Conclusion – A Review of the Dynamics of the Nuclear Energy Industry: Strategy Development for the Nuclear Energy Sector

8.1 Introduction

The vital components of a nuclear energy strategy are detailed here, building on Chapters 2–7. A nuclear new build strategy matrix is formulated from the deconstruction of energy law and policy in the previous analysis. This new nuclear development strategy matrix has four major components:

1. A willing state/government – generally this takes the form of having cross-party political support.
2. Effective public administration and project management.
3. The 'key drivers' of energy policy and legislation – this includes the incentives guaranteed by legislation.
4. The project partner, i.e. the company generally which is providing the technology.

This text has reviewed the dynamics of the nuclear energy industry in the twenty-first century and aims to deconstruct the energy law and policy in the area and establish what are the key components to successful policy delivery. It involved a comparative analysis of the United States, and the EU where two countries were analysed, Romania and the United Kingdom.

The period covered in the research is from 1990 to 2010 for both Romania and the US, and from 2002 to 2012 for the UK. The following section explores some of the specific lessons learned across Romania, the UK and the US. Then it draws some comparisons across the three countries and details the emergent strategies in the nuclear industry in all three countries. Except where specified, the nuclear energy industry refers to the part of the industry that develops (and then operates) nuclear new build and includes the supply chain.

In deconstructing energy law and policy in relation to the nuclear energy sector, an emergent strategy for successful energy law and policy delivery can be established. This strategy may apply to other sectors in the energy sector and this is an area for future research. In identifying the key components of energy law and policy in relation to nuclear energy, a three-step process is followed to advance a strategy for the sector. The first step involves identifying the key drivers and vital components of a nuclear energy strategy; the second develops a new nuclear development strategy matrix; the third conducts a country analysis using this new nuclear development strategy matrix.

8.2   Lessons learned specifically from Romania, the US and the UK

Romania planned nuclear new build has made progress amidst the turbulence the country has experienced in recent decades. The transition period to EU membership was not without controversy, and there still remain question marks over the operation of some of the Romanian democratic institutional structures. Nevertheless, despite the political, economic and social upheaval in Romania, it has successfully established a nuclear power programme. The research on Romania highlights many lessons for emerging civil nuclear energy nations regarding the problems, issues and considerations that they will have to address to develop a safe and operational nuclear energy plant on time and on budget.

Nuclear energy policy was assessed across three states in the **United States** – Georgia, Pennsylvania, and Texas – in 1990–2010. New insights are provided through the unique comparison of these three US states that have deregulated, regulated and 'hybrid' electricity markets. It is evident that law can play a central role in the nuclear energy sector, and that policy in the nuclear energy sector can become state-driven. The research adds to the literature on public administration, legal development and that on nuclear energy policy. Also examined, from a policy perspective, was US Federal policy inaction and contradiction in the nuclear energy sector from 1990 to 2010. As befits policy research, it was necessary to engage with many disciplines (for example, law and politics), and hence the contributions move beyond that of nuclear energy policy literature and in particular to that on nuclear new build and other assessments of large infrastructure projects. A review was undertaken of the nuclear renaissance in the US, which concluded that it had not transpired by 2010.

The focus was on planned nuclear new build in the *United Kingdom*. As a new nuclear energy programme begins again in the UK, the research focused on five key issues in the nuclear new build process: (1) law, policy and development; (2) public administration; (3) project management; (4) the economics of nuclear; and (5) safety and education. In order to achieve a sustainable nuclear energy policy, these issues are of major importance. Further, it is demonstrated that policy in the area remains unresolved, in particular at an institutional and legal level. However, contrary to the literature in some areas, the research identified a change of course as the UK concentrates on delivering a long-term policy for the nuclear energy sector and the overall energy sector.

8.3   The dynamics of the nuclear energy industry and outlook for the future

There are lessons that can be deduced from the resulting analysis of the three countries. This section analyses three themes that emerge from a comparative analysis of the three countries: (1) understanding the industry dynamic; (2) the presence of a policy; and (3) towards a strategy for nuclear new build.

8.3.1   Understanding the industry dynamic

There are misunderstandings of how the nuclear energy industry was evolving or the expected rate of evolution. The industry has taken a gradual process to development rather than its previous rapid development from the 1950s to 1980s. Development now takes place on an individual project basis rather than on a programme basis. This is what makes UK nuclear energy policy significant, in that there is a full programme for nuclear development planned with eight reactors in the current new build programme, though what materialises is another matter. It is, as the research suggests, the case that the nuclear energy industry is more suited to developing on a programme basis: only then can the benefits begin to accrue, as the learning curve will reduce costs. Unfortunately for the nuclear energy industry, many countries do not view developing the industry in this way: successful completion of a new nuclear reactor is viewed as a successful project. Consequently, this means that the nuclear energy industry worldwide has been evolving to development on a project-by-project basis. This is why the industry has been shrinking in the EU and US and why there is an expected further reduction in the number of companies that can build a nuclear power plant.

In both **Romania and the US**, the nuclear energy industry continues, but on a project-by-project basis. This approach has its problems as it restricts which companies will deliver the project. There has to be some level of financial incentive given to the company, usually in the form of: a direct incentive, as a result of new legislation; a high possibility of benefiting from a learning curve so that costs will be reduced for the next project; and/or long-term contracts available for the sale of the electricity. In Romania the state operator (Nuclearelectrica) was essentially restricted to continuing with AECL to deliver the project at Cernavoda even though some overtures were made to other companies. The development of plans for new nuclear projects in Romania has slowed down and some of the investors in the project have withdrawn. Further, AECL has experienced some problems in its home country, Canada, where the government sold the commercial reactor business to SNC-Lavalin (the agreement was eventually signed in October 2011) and it is now called Candu Energy Inc.

In the **US**, plans across the country after the Energy Policy Act 2005 increased in abundance. However, the legislation, in addition to being unclear, was set to encourage only the first few reactors to be built rather than the possible programme of nuclear development that could have occurred (based on initial interest following the 2005 legislation). As a result only a few projects have been initiated, and these are in Georgia and South Carolina. Of importance here is that in Georgia, nuclear developers are given direct incentives through state law in addition to the Federal incentives. Further, the companies involved are the same for both states, and hence they will have the added advantage of reducing costs as they move along the learning curve from the first reactor build project. Finally, long-term contracts for the electricity are available since both states are regulated.

The **UK**, in contrast to Romania and the US, is still in the planning phase of its latest nuclear programme, which is prompted by the potential closure of its existing reactor fleet. It has moved forward on all three issues, and the legislation to offer incentives and long-term contracts are 'works in progress' in terms of application; however, the legislation has been introduced in the form of the Energy Act 2013. However, the plan for developing eight nuclear reactors, a programme rather than individual nuclear energy projects, is unclear. It is not currently evident if a company can reduce its costs from benefiting from the learning curve. This is because the UK government sold off the sites for the proposed reactors, as a result of which they have gone to separate companies. This had meant that EDF (a French company) and RWE and EoN (German companies) owned two sites each. This has reduced the scope for companies to benefit from reduced costs via the learning curve. In essence, the UK divided its programme for nuclear development into projects, and this has decreased its attractiveness for investment by the private sector. Earlier, for these reasons and also because of business development and strategic concerns in their home nation, RWE and EoN announced their intention to withdraw from the UK nuclear energy industry and this culminated in the sale to Hitachi. There is a similarity here with Romania, and it is instrumental who the partners are in a nuclear project because conditions in the home country of a company can seriously affect the development of the industry. This also raises the similar point that if one of the three internal industry conditions is not there – (1) understanding of the industry dynamic; (2) the presence of a policy; and (3) a strategy for nuclear new build exists – this limits who can build a nuclear project in a country. This is why the UK policy process has resulted in Hitachi planning to build there. This is primarily because it can benefit from the learning curve as it has built the reactor type (ABWR) before and also it sees the move as a strategic investment. There has nevertheless been a serious setback to the industry as it will take Hitachi an estimated three to four years to gain licence approval for the ABWR reactor (though it has been approved in the US already).

8.3.2   The presence of a policy

The second major point of comparison concerns the presence of a nuclear energy policy. An examination of this has important considerations for the outlook of the nuclear energy industry in the three countries. Under the term 'energy policy', the research recognises three vital components: public administration, project management, and cross-party political support. These are three vital components for a successful nuclear energy policy to be present.

In all three countries the importance of having a nuclear energy policy has wavered over the last two decades. In *Romania*, having an energy policy has been of central importance, mainly, in order to decrease its reliance on Russia. As part of this policy to increase its own energy independence, it was vital to finish the reactors at Cernavoda. This was achieved for two of these reactors, and as part of an energy plan that has notably had cross-party political support. A clear nuclear energy plan was developed in Romania which has ambitions to be similar to France in terms of aiming to rely on nuclear energy for the vast majority of its electricity needs. However, the absence of some of the key factors – public administration and project management – that are vital for a successful policy have slowed down these policy aims and continue to do so in Romania.

As stated in the research on **Romania**, its public administration system remains a work in progress. This has contributed to an unclear direction of where the nuclear energy industry will go after the Cernavoda project, and also makes it unattractive for some foreign investors. With a second nuclear project proposed, there have been delays within the public administration system to the approval of this project. This, and the decrease in the attractiveness of investment in the nuclear energy industry in Romania, have seen a number of investors (French GDF Suez, Spanish Iberdrola, Germany's RWE and Czech CEZ) pull out of their involvement in financing Cernavoda 3 and 4. Further, problems have arisen because AECL, the key partner with which the reactors were to be built, has had its own problems in Canada. This has caused a major delay to the nuclear energy industry in Romania. The problem arises in Romania that its nuclear energy policy, while being long-term in its orientation, is not managed like a programme of development. Instead, Cernavoda 3 and 4 are seen as a separate development to subsequent nuclear new builds. This decreases the attractiveness for companies to be involved in the Cernavoda project, and unfortunately no progress will be made on the new four-reactor project until Cernavoda is complete. This division of its programme for development of the nuclear energy industry demonstrates a misunderstanding of where good project management actually starts. As argued in this research, it begins when policy is formulated – that is when planning for a project begins – whether it be a public or private project. While Romania has a nuclear energy policy that is agreed upon by all political parties, it has yet to have the benefit of a good public management system to deliver it, and an understanding of project management to develop it.

The *US*, in contrast to the Romania and the UK, has successfully brought about new nuclear build from its recent energy policy. However, as mentioned earlier, this was as a result of other drivers at state level rather than Federal level. Nevertheless, in comparison to the UK and similarly to Romania, the US recognised the need for a coherent and inclusive energy policy. This legislation even has the word 'policy' in its name – not a common phenomenon in legislative naming, though a process continued from previous energy legislation in the US: the Energy Policy Act of 2005 (hereafter also referred to as the '2005 Act'). This legislation offered varied incentivised schemes for the different forms of energy, and in essence is the model of what the UK is attempting with its own Energy Act 2013. However, the three vital components of good public administration, project management and cross-party political support, have not always been present. This has resulted in delays in the response of the nuclear energy industry to begin construction of a nuclear power plant, and it remains unclear as to what the long-term plan for the industry is.

The 2005 Act in the *US* has been significant for nuclear energy in terms of the incentives it has offered, with the most prominent of these being the loan guarantee system. However, to date, only one state, Georgia, has benefited from the loan guarantees system. Overall, despite the surge of eighteen applications to build new nuclear projects after the 2005 Act, the legislation has taken years to implement. Further, the amount stated to be available under the loan guarantee system has been demonstrated to be significantly too low. This is because the 2005 Act allowed for $18.5 billion for loan guarantees, with the Georgia project claiming nearly $6.5 billion of this total. Hence, it is likely that only two projects will be able to use the loan guarantee system, based on the amount already allocated to the Georgia project. It is because of this that the Obama administration debated and sought (unsuccessfully) an increase of up to $36 billion in 2010 (Chu 2010) and $54.5 billion in 2011 (Holt 2011). These factors highlight that the public administration system in the US was unsure as to the exact aim for the nuclear energy industry in the long-term. They misunderstood whether the nuclear energy policy was to support a project or a programme of development.

In contrast to Romania and the UK, there is no cross-party political support in the US. Hence, as stated, attempts to add to the amount available under the loan guarantee system have failed primarily because of party politics rather than because of differing policy options. The US has had major success with its 2005 Act, a triumph for the public administration system, but it has failed to successfully implement the resulting policies into practice with respect to the nuclear energy industry. The legislation failed to incorporate the in-built flexibility that would have seen more of the eighteen applications which followed the publication of the Act succeed. Indeed, were it not for state policies in Georgia and South Carolina (where construction did begin in 2013 at Vogtle-3 and Virgil C Summer-2, respectively), it is unlikely that the 2005 Act would yet have delivered any beginnings of new construction in the nuclear energy industry. Good project management begins at this policy and legislation formulation stage, and this was not recognised in the US or in Romania as stated earlier.

The **UK** in contrast has had no encompassing energy policy, although it had a decade of legislation and policy documents from 2002. It is only in the latter few years that it has tried to bring everything together, and this resulted in the Energy Act 2013. It is similar to the 2005 Act in the US; however, it is yet to be applied, so one can only speculate as to whether it will deliver new nuclear new build. One distinct advantage, however, is that the UK has stated that its aim is to have eight new nuclear reactors, and it has identified and sold off prospective new nuclear sites. This is significant in that the UK recognises there is something to be gained from a programme of delivery rather than just a project. However, this latter issue is where the plan runs into difficulty.

The Energy Act 2013 seems to follow the US 2005 Act in allocating some incentives for those who may be first to build. This is a mistake unless a programme of nuclear power plants is being planned. In the UK, however, there is such a programme, but it consists of different companies building various parts of it. Companies that come later to the programme will have large upfront costs to pay and will not have developed a learning curve; the earlier companies will not share theirs for obvious commercial reasons. Hence, the attraction of developing the later stages of the UK nuclear power programme are reduced, and a later company will be at a significant disadvantage, with fewer incentives and also the cost of developing a new learning curve. Hence, only particular companies can build the later parts of the programme: part of the reason Hitachi has chosen to build in the UK is that it has already built the reactor type before and hence its learning curve costs will be reduced. The public administration system in the UK is learning fast but as yet there remains – as in the US and Romania – a point of *disconnection* in terms of understanding where the planning or project management begins for the nuclear energy sector. It begins at the policy and legislation formulation stage, and hence there remains an opportunity in the UK to rectify its approach to developing the nuclear energy sector.

As in Romania, there is now cross-political party support for nuclear energy and in general for a UK energy policy. This is a situation that should be fully utilised by the public administration system, and questions have to be raised over the exact ambitions of UK energy policy and indeed nuclear energy policy. Legal and policy certainty is crucial to investment in the nuclear energy industry, as demonstrated in both the US and Romania, and it is rather novel in the UK to have the cross-party political support to bring that legal and policy certainty into existence. However, some commendable work has been completed by the public administration system in the UK, through the key development of the new Office for Nuclear Development (OND) in the energy sector. In essence, the OND has become the project manager of the UK nuclear energy industry, and it has placed an emphasis on the nuclear energy value chain where it has actively encouraged and incentivised the UK companies to enter it. This should aid development of the UK nuclear sector over the longer term, and Hitachi has already signed preliminary agreements with Babcock International and Rolls-Royce. For any country that aspires to have a nuclear programme, the OND is probably an institution that could be replicated and both Romania and the US would have reason to benefit from the establishment of a similar institution.

8.3.3   Emergent strategy for nuclear new build

The research has highlighted several key issues when comparing the three countries and exploring the outlook for the future in these countries. These factors are highlighted in Table 8.1 as being key drivers, and vital components of a nuclear energy strategy.

As a result of the research conducted and the conclusions drawn from a three-country comparison, it is possible to advance a nuclear new build strategy matrix. This matrix takes into account key characteristics of a nuclear new build strategy. It can inform a state-owned enterprise or private company on the possibility of success in its nuclear new build plans or new build plans for a particular country – see Figure 8.1. The aim in each quadrant is to be as close as possible

Table 8.1 Key drivers and vital components of a nuclear energy strategy

Issue	Elements
Understanding the industry dynamic: the key drivers	A financial incentive given to the company with this usually taking the form of a direct incentive as a result of new legislation
	A high possibility of benefiting from a learning curve so costs will be reduced for the next project
	Long-term contracts are available for the sale of the electricity
The presence of a policy: the vital components	Public administration
	Project management
	Cross-party political support

Source: Compiled by the author (2013)

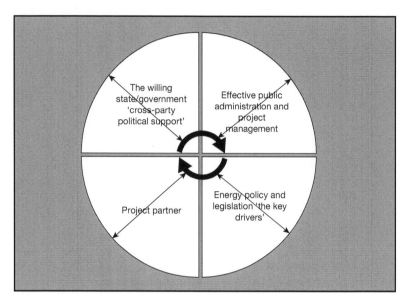

Figure 8.1 A nuclear new build strategy matrix

to the end of the arrow towards the centre-point. The further down the arrow away from the centre-point the characteristics of a country are in each quadrant, the more difficult it will be to realise a nuclear new build project in that particular country. There are four key elements to the nuclear new build strategy matrix:

1. A willing state/government – generally this takes the form of having cross-party political support.
2. Effective public administration and project management.
3. The 'key drivers' of energy policy and legislation – this includes the incentives guaranteed by legislation.
4. The project partner, i.e. the company generally which is providing the technology.

The matrix in Figure 8.1 can be considered for each country, as detailed in Table 8.2. This strategic analysis gives an overview of what the future for nuclear new build is in each country and summarises what has been discussed in the earlier parts of the section. It is evident that a key finding is that the nuclear energy industry is in a state of transition, and the conclusions are given in the following section.

Table 8.2 Country analysis using the nuclear new build strategy matrix

Strategy matrix element	Country	Analysis
Willing state/ government 'cross-party political support'	Romania	Present
	UK	Present
	US	Not present at Federal level but is at state level in some states
Effective public administration and project management	Romania	Improvement needed, a major focus on policy delivery needed
	UK	Getting there, and the new Office for Nuclear Development a major addition
	US	Further towards the centre-point than the UK or Romania, but slow implementation of policy and low policy flexibility and poor project management are concerns
Energy policy and legislation 'the key drivers'	Romania	Has a clear energy policy but weak in legislation, incentives and long-term policy aims need to be re-examined
	UK	Currently in the process of making some final amendments to the Energy Act 2013, but there remains concern over the effectiveness of the incentives and the ambitions for the nuclear energy industry
	US	The legislation is in place, but limited incentives have been offered, and no clear long-term goal for the nuclear energy industry has emerged
Project partner (generally, the technology provider)	Romania	Romania has been hampered by its main project partner AECL having issues in its home nation where, since 2011, it has changed into private partnership

Table 8.2 (*cont.*)		
Strategy matrix element	**Country**	**Analysis**
	UK	Has divided up the nuclear development programme, and lost the second stage partner because of home nation concerns (RWE and EoN) before Hitachi agreed to take over
	US	The nuclear energy industry is developing on a project-by-project basis and undoubtedly Westinghouse will play a lead role as it is involved in both projects in Georgia and South Carolina

8.4   Conclusion

The energy industry is changing and is being driven by an energy strategy centred on a move towards low-carbon technology. In some countries, and in particular the countries studied here, national governments see that nuclear energy has a role to play in this strategy. There have been developments since the research was finalised. In Romania, the project at Cernavoda 3 and 4 has stalled with the economic crisis prompting some of the investors to pull out of the project. There is currently a search for new partners. Most significantly, in the US, the NRC has granted a construction and operating licence (COL) to Southern Nuclear. Consequently, the project at Plant Vogtle is the first to be awarded a licence in twenty-eight years in the US and the two reactors planned are expected to be completed and in operation in 2016 and 2017. In the UK nuclear new build projects are developing at a slower pace. EDF is expected to build the first at Hinkley Point C. The planned date is around 2020; however, as identified earlier, of significance is the outcome of the electricity market reform, a process not expected to be completed until 2014–15 (at the earliest before the law is applied).

The three countries analysed in this research can learn from progress made in China and South Korea on building nuclear reactors on time and on budget. This is an area of potential further exploration (although data and personal access may prove challenging). The nuclear energy industry is already examining how other industries try to meet their time and financial deadlines, and this learning process needs to include a global evaluation of nuclear new build projects.

This book ends at a point of great uncertainty in the territories considered and this is why this study is helpful and timely. The complex policy issues in nuclear energy are not dead historically, and they demonstrate a significant residual uncertainty that pre-dated the incident at Fukushima. The examination into the different countries reveals that a variety of key policy issues remain unresolved and, where a consensus has not yet been reached, these factors inhibit the growth of the nuclear energy industry. Nevertheless, the research advances an emergent strategy for the development of new nuclear energy projects that, if followed, can potentially resolve the uncertainty and result in the successful development of new energy infrastructure. Further, its application to the development of other energy infrastructure can be explored.

Appendix: Interview Codes for Interviews Conducted

Interview codes identify with the institution, with personal names being kept private. The author remains responsible for all errors in data collection, and wording of quotes and attribution to the sources.

Chapter 4 codes: Romania

Romania interviewees

Interview code	Organisation
I-1	CITON
I-2	CITON
I-3	CITON
I-4	CITON
I-5	Nuclearelectrica
I-6	Nuclearelectrica
I-7	Elcomex
I-8	European Union
I-9	Euratom
I-10	Polytechnic of Bucharest
I-11	Korea Hydro & Nuclear Power
I-12	RWE
I-13	Herbert Smith

Chapter 5 codes: United States

Georgia interviewees

Interview code	Organisation
GI-1	Georgia State Senate
GI-2	Georgia Public Service Commission
GI-3	Southern Company

Interview code	Organisation
GI-4	Southern Company
GI-5	Georgia Department of Natural Resources – Environmental Protection Division, Environmental Radiation Program
GI-6	SERC Reliability Corporation
GI-7	Georgia Public Service Commission
GI-8	Center of Innovation for Energy, Georgia Environmental Finance Authority (GEFA)
GI-9	Southern Alliance for Clean Energy
GI-10	Georgia Institute of Technology, & Oak Ridge National Laboratory
GI-11	Emory Law School, Emory University, Atlanta

Pennsylvania interviewees

Interview code	Organisation
PI-1	Pennsylvania State Senate
PI-2	Pennsylvania State Senate
PI-3	Pennsylvania State House of Representatives
PI-4	Pennsylvania State House of Representatives
PI-5	Pennsylvania State House of Representatives
PI-6	Pennsylvania Department of Environmental Protection
PI-7	Pennsylvania Department of Environmental Protection
PI-8	Pennsylvania Public Utility Commission
PI-9	PJM Interconnection, LLC
PI-10	Office of Attorney General – Pennsylvania
PI-11	Tepper School of Business, and Engineering and Public Policy, Carnegie Mellon University, PA
PI-12	Tepper School of Business, and Engineering and Public Policy, Carnegie Mellon University, PA

Interview code	Organisation
PI-13	Department of Energy and Mineral Engineering, and Electricity Markets Initiative Pennsylvania State University – Electricity Centre
PI-14	Center for Energy, Enterprise and the Environment, Penn Future
PI-15	Citizen Power (PA)
PI-16	PPL – Susquehanna Energy PA
PI-17	Exelon

Texas interviewees

Interview code	Organisation
TI–1	Texas State Senate
TI-2	Texas State House of Representatives
TI-3	Texas State House of Representatives
TI-4	Public Utility Commission
TI-5	Public Utility Commission
TI-6	Texas Comptroller of Public Accounts
TI-7	Office of Attorney General
TI-8	Office of Public Utility Counsel, Texas
TI-9	ERCOT, Texas
TI-10	Austin Energy
TI-11	San Antonio Energy (CPS)
TI-12	NRG Texas LLC
TI-13	Exelon
TI-14	South Texas Project Nuclear Operating Company
TI-15	Former Luminant/Energy Start-Up (TX) – Clean Energy Technology Association
TI-16	Environmental Defense Fund

Interview code	Organisation
TI-17	Center for International Energy & Environmental Policy, LBJ School of Public Affairs, The University of Texas at Austin
TI-18	Center for International Energy & Environmental Policy, LBJ School of Public Affairs, The University of Texas at Austin
TI-19	Cockrell School of Engineering, The University of Texas at Austin
TI-20	Institute for Fusion Studies, The University of Texas at Austin

Chapter 6 codes: United States

Category 1: Elected politicians – state politicians on state legislature energy committees

Interview code	Organisation
1A	Georgia State Senate
1B	Pennsylvania State Senate
1C	Pennsylvania State Senate
1D	Pennsylvania State House of Representatives
1E	Pennsylvania State House of Representatives
1F	Pennsylvania State House of Representatives
1G	Texas State Senate
1H	Texas State House of Representatives
1I	Texas State House of Representatives

Category 2: Public sector – federal and state agencies: Finance, Environment, Energy and Nuclear Safety, State Electricity Regulator, State Transmission Grid System

Interview code	Organisation
2A	Office of Nuclear Energy, US Department of Energy
2B	US Nuclear Regulatory Commission

Interview code	Organisation
2C	US Nuclear Regulatory Commission
2D	Georgia Public Service Commission
2E	Georgia Department of Natural Resources – Environmental Protection Division, Environmental Radiation Program
2F	SERC Reliability Corporation
2G	Georgia Public Service Commission
2H	Center of Innovation for Energy. Georgia Environmental Finance Authority (GEFA)
2I	Pennsylvania Department of Environmental Protection
2J	Pennsylvania Department of Environmental Protection
2K	Pennsylvania Public Utility Commission
2L	PJM Interconnection, LLC
2M	Office of Attorney General – Pennsylvania
2N	Public Utility Commission
2O	Public Utility Commission
2P	Texas Comptroller of Public Accounts
2Q	Office of Attorney General
2R	Office of Public Utility Counsel, Texas
2S	ERCOT, Texas

Category 3: Nuclear energy companies

Interview code	Organisation
3A	Southern Company
3B	Southern Company
3C	PPL – Susquehanna Energy PA
3D	Exelon
3E	Austin Energy

Interview code	Organisation
3F	San Antonio Energy (CPS)
3G	NRG Texas LLC
3H	Exelon
3I	South Texas Project Nuclear Operating Company

Category 4: Academic researchers

Interview code	Organisation
4A	Department of Nuclear Science and Engineering, MIT
4B	Department of Nuclear Science and Engineering, MIT
4C	MIT Laboratory for Energy and the Environment, MIT
4D	Department of Physics, MIT
4E	John F. Kennedy School of Government, Harvard University
4F	Department of Economics, Stanford University
4G	Georgia Institute of Technology, & Oak Ridge National Laboratory
4H	Emory Law School, Emory University, Atlanta
4I	Center for International Energy & Environmental Policy, LBJ School of Public Affairs, The University of Texas at Austin
4J	Center for International Energy & Environmental Policy, LBJ School of Public Affairs, The University of Texas at Austin
4K	Cockrell School of Engineering, The University of Texas at Austin
4L	Institute for Fusion Studies, The University of Texas at Austin
4M	Tepper School of Business, and Engineering and Public Policy, Carnegie Mellon University, PA

Interview code	Organisation
4N	Tepper School of Business, and Engineering and Public Policy, Carnegie Mellon University, PA
4O	Department of Energy and Mineral Engineering, and Electricity Markets Initiative Pennsylvania State University – Electricity Centre

Category 5: Non-governmental organisations

Interview code	Organisation
5A	Public Citizen
5B	Nuclear Energy Institute
5C	Center for Energy, Enterprise and the Environment, Penn Future
5D	Citizen Power (PA)
5E	Former Luminant/Energy Start-Up (TX) – Clean Energy Technology Association
5F	Environmental Defense Fund
5G	Southern Alliance for Clean Energy

Chapter 7 codes: United Kingdom

Stakeholders identified and interviewed for the UK research

Interview code	Organisation
State institutions/public sector interviewees – interview code for category: A-PS	
1A	DECC Office for Nuclear Development, Office for Nuclear Regulation
2A	Nuclear Decommissioning Authority
3A	Office for Nuclear Regulation

Interview code	Organisation
4A	European Commission
5A	Euratom, European Commission

Industry private sector interviewees – interview code for category: B-PRS

1B	Westinghouse
2B	Areva UK
3B	Eversheds
4B	Atkins
5B	39 Essex Street Chambers
6B	EDF

Academic researcher interviewees – interview code for category: C-AR

1C	Oxford Energy Institute
2C	Oxford Energy Institute
3C	Cambridge Nuclear Energy Centre, University of Cambridge
4C	Lancaster University
5C	University of Manchester and Rolls-Royce
6C	Cranfield University
7C	Warwick University
8C	University of Greenwich

Global institution and NGO interviewees – interview code for category: D-NGO

1D	Nuclear Industry Association
2D	World Nuclear Association
3D	Independent Nuclear Researcher (1)
4D	Independent Nuclear Researcher (2)
5D	Chatham House

Notes

Chapter 1

1. This was particularly the view in the UK with the coal strikes and the British dependency on coal.
2. See the history of NATO, available on the NATO website *http://www. nato.int/history/nato-history.html* (last accessed December 2011).
3. Its special status is not just restricted to the EU but also to other non-EU countries that have nuclear power.

Chapter 2

1. Then part of the Soviet Union.
2. The major accident at the Chernobyl nuclear plant in the Ukraine in 1986 led to numerous deaths (thirty-one immediate deaths and the evacuation of 135,000 people and widespread radioactive contamination, thus giving way to a worldwide fear of nuclear power and casting doubts on its safety (*New York Times* 1987; NEA 1995; Robbins 1997). This was preceded by the accident at Three Mile Island in the United States in 1979 which resulted in no deaths but many legal class action cases (Moss and Sills, 1981; Sovacool 2008).
3. The following studies have a one country focus: (UK) Tweena (2006); Davies (1984); Wynne (1982); (France) Hecht (1998); (US) Pope (2008); (Sweden) Nohrstedt (2005, 2008, 2009).

Chapter 4

1. Romania Statistical Yearbook 2009, National Institute of Statistics, Bucharest, Romania.
2. The political parties in Romania are: Social Democratic Party (PSD), Democratic-Liberal Party (PD-L), National Liberal Party (PNL), Democratic Union of the Hungarian Minority (UDMR) and Greater Romania Party (PRM).
3. It was established under its own international treaty, the IAEA statute.

4. In 1955, the Non-Aligned Movement (NAM) was founded and the first meeting held in Bandung, Indonesia. The role of the new organisation was clear. In a world still recovering from the Second World War, the Soviet Union and United States had embarked on a new kind of military and political confrontation: the Cold War. The place of a NAM was to keep the two opposite blocs in equilibrium and prevent the Cold War from turning hot (Caragea 2009). After the fall of communism and the dissolution of the Warsaw Pact in 1991, NAM seemed out of place in a world and there have been calls for the organisation to disband but it remains in existence.

5. Romania after the Second World War was initially influenced politically by the Soviet Union. This continued under the rule of Nicolae Ceausescu, the new leader of the newly formed national Communist party after the Soviet troops left in 1958. Ceausescu looked eastwards in terms of controlling Romania, and at the heart of his governance was Stalinist authoritarianism. A mixed style then emerged influenced by North Korea's leader Kim II Sung (Tolnay 2002) in the 1970s and 1980s.

6. In 2009 Romania was 20 per cent energy dependent, i.e. reliant on exports, mostly from Russia (Eurostat 2011).

7. Magurele was a purpose-built town designed to accommodate nuclear activities and to accommodate the staff at the various research centres.

8. See United Nations (2006) report on 'Romania's experience on the relationship between the competition authority and the sector regulators' prepared for the United Nations Conference on Trade and Development, November 2006.

9. Established by Decree No. 29 of 8 January 1990.

10. Now the Canadian Nuclear Safety Commission (CNSC).

11. As well as for quality assurance, radiation safety, safeguards, radioactive waste management, import and export of nuclear installations and nuclear materials, physical protection, on-site emergency preparedness and early notification to all potentially affected States, and the IAEA in the event of a nuclear accident or radiological emergency.

12. There have been several amendments since, with the latest being Law No. 193 of 13 May 2003.

13. For example, Nuclearelectrica received €27.7 million, accounting for 90.6 per cent of funds allocated to the budget of the Ministry of Economy and Commerce (MEC) in 2006. Further, the Ministry of Finance gave an emergency €10 million loan for construction works

currently underway on the second reactor. The Romanian Authority for Nuclear Activities and the Bucharest Uranium National Company each received €1.154 million, the MEC announced. (*Romanian Daily*, 2006).

14. In fact, Government Ordinance No. 7/2003 established the National Nuclear Plan (*Planul Nuclear National – PNN*), and elaborated on the '2002 strategy'. This strategy is designed to establish the long-term objectives for the nuclear sector of Romania and envisages a significant portion of electricity generation to be from nuclear.

Chapter 5

1. These numbers signify the interviewee and their respective state, such that: the first Georgian interview is (GI-1), the second (GI-2), the first Pennsylvanian interview (PI-1) and the first Texan interview (TI-1), and so on. For the list of interviewees, see the Appendix.

2. Energy Information Administration (EIA) (2010). Annual Energy Outlook 2010 with Projections to 2035. US Nuclear Power Plants: Continued life or replacement after 60.

3. Ibid. 69.

4. See the Nuclear Regulatory Commission website for this information and updates to these statistics: http://www.nrc.gov/reactors/operating/licensing/renewal.html (last accessed August 2011).

Overall note

Parts of Chapter 3 have been based on a publication: Heffron, R. J. (2012), 'Lessons from the United States: for legal change and delay in energy law in the United Kingdom', *International Energy Law Review*, 31 (2), 71–7.

Parts of Chapter 4 have been based on a publication: Heffron, R. J. (2012), 'Romanian nuclear new build: progress amid turbulence', *Progress in Nuclear Energy*, 56, 43–60.

Parts of Chapter 5 have been based on a publication: Heffron, R. J. (2013), 'Lessons for nuclear new build in the USA 1990–2010: a three state analysis', *Technology Forecasting and Social Change*, 80 (5), 876–92.

Parts of Chapter 6 have been based on a publication: Heffron, R. J. (2013), 'Nuclear energy policy in the United States 1990–2010: a federal or state responsibility', *Energy Policy*, 64, 254–66.

Parts of Chapter 7 have been based on a publication: Heffron, R. J. (2013), 'The application of contrast explanation to energy policy research: UK nuclear energy policy 2002–2012', *Energy Policy*, 55, 602–16.

This note is to acknowledge these journals for permitting the use of this material and thanks are expressed to the publishers of these journals.

References and Bibliography

Aaker, D. A., Stayman, D. M. and Hagerty, M. R. (1986), 'Warmth in advertising: measurement, impact, and sequence effects', *The Journal of Consumer Research*, 12 (4), 365–81.

Aberbach, J. and Rockman, B. (2002), 'Conducting and coding elite interviews', *Political Science and Politics Society*, 35 (4), 673–6.

Aherne, J. F. (2011), 'Prospects for nuclear energy', *Energy Economics*, 33 (2011) 572–80.

Akerlof, G. A. (1970) 'The market for "lemons": quality uncertainty and the market mechanism', *Quarterly Journal of Economics*, 84 (3), 488–500.

Altshuler, A. and Luberoff, D. (2003), *Mega-Projects: The Changing Politics of Urban Public Investment*, Washington DC: Brookings Institution.

American Planning Association, (2005), 'JAPA article calls on planners to help end inaccuracies in public project revenue forecasting', available online http://www.planning.org/newsreleases/2005/ftp040705.html (last accessed October 2011).

Applied Decision Analysis Inc. (1983), *An Analysis of Power Plant Construction Leadtimes*. EPRI-2880, vol. 1, Palo Alto, CA: Electric Power Research Institute.

Argyris, C. and Schon, D. (1978), *Organisational Learning: A Theory of Action Perspective*, San Francisco, CA: Jossey-Bass.

Arias, A. D. and van Beers, C. (2010), 'Environmentally damaging government policies in the energy sector', in van Geenhuizen, M., Nuttall, W. J., Gibson, D. V. and Oftedal, E. M., *Energy and Innovation: Structural Change and Policy Implications*, Indiana: Purdue University Press.

Aristotle (2011), *Ethics*, Book 1.C.4, trans. Bartlett, R. C. and Collins, S. D., Chicago: The University of Chicago Press.

Ash J. (2010), 'New nuclear energy, risk and justice: regulatory strategies for an era of limited trust', *Politics and Policy*, 38 (2), 255–84.

ASM Bresica SpA v Comune di Rodengo Saiano (C-347/06) [2008] ECR I-5641.

Atomic Energy Act 1954 s. 170 Pub.L. 83–703.

Aucoin, P. and Neintzman, R. (2000), 'The dialectics of accountability for performance in public management reform', *International Review of Administrative Sciences*, 66, 44–55.

Baker, K. and Stoker, G. (2011), 'Metagovernance and the UK nuclear industry – a limiting case', in Torfing, J. and Triantafillou, P. (eds), *Interactive Policy Making, Metagovernance and Democracy*, Colchester: ECPR – Studies in European Political Science.

Barker Review of Land Use Planning (2006), Norwich: HMSO.

Bernstein, R. J. (1976), *The Restructuring of Social and Political Theory*, Philadelphia, PA: The University of Pennsylvania Press.

Bircham, Dyson and Bell, LLP (BDB) (2009), *A Practical Guide to National Infrastructure Projects*, London: Butterworth.

Blue Ribbon Commission (BRC) (2011), Blue Ribbon Commission on America's Nuclear Future: Report to the Secretary of Energy, Washington, DC: US Department of Energy.

Blumsack, S. (2007), 'Measuring the benefits and costs of regional electric grid integration', *Energy Law Journal*, 28, 147–84.

Bouquet, A. (2003), 'How current are Euratom provisions on nuclear supply and ownership in view of the European Union's enlargement?' *Nuclear Law Bulletin*, 68, 7–38.

Bradford, P. A. (2009), 'The nuclear renaissance meets economic reality', *Bulletin of the Atomic Scientists*, 65 (6), 60–4.

Bredimas, A. and Nuttall, W. J. (2008), 'An international comparison of regulatory organizations and licensing procedures for new nuclear power plants', *Energy Policy*, 36, 1344–54.

Breyer, S. (1978), '*Vermont Yankee* and the courts' role in the nuclear energy controversy', *Harvard Law Review*, 91, 1833, 1977–8.

British Energy (2011), Sizewell B, available from http://www.british-energy.com/pagetemplate.php?pid=96 (last accessed December 2011).

Bruggink, J. J. C. and Van der Zwaan, B. C. C. (2002), 'The role of nuclear energy in establishing sustainable energy paths', *International Journal of Global Energy Issues*, vol. 18, no. 2–4.

Bryman, A. (2004), *Social Research Methods*, 2nd edn, Oxford: Oxford University Press.

Burnham, P., Gilland, K., Grant, W. and Layton-Henry, Z. (2004), *Research Methods in Politics*, Basingstoke: Macmillan.

Cabinet Office (2002), The Energy Review, Cabinet Office Performance and Innovation Unit, London: The Stationery Office.

Cabinet Office (2009), The Road to 2010: Addressing the Nuclear Question in the Twenty First Century, Cm 7675.

Calinescu, M., Georgescu, V. and Tismaneanu, V. (1991), *Romanians: A History*, Ohio: Ohio State University Press.

Cameron, P, D. (2007), 'The revival of nuclear power: an analysis of the legal implications', *Journal of Environmental Law*, 19 (1), 71–87.

Campbell, J. L. (1988), *Collapse of an Industry: Nuclear Power and the Contradictions of US Policy*, New York: Cornell University Press.

Cantor, R. and Hewlett, J. (1988), 'The economics of nuclear power. Further evidence on learning, economies of scale, and regulatory effects', *Resources and Energy*, 10, 315–35.

Carley, S. (2011), 'The era of State energy policy innovation: A review of policy instruments', *Review of Policy Research*, 28 (3), 265–94.

Carlson, J. M. (1990), 'Subjective ideological similarity between candidates and supporters: a study of party elites', *Political Psychology*, 11 (3), 485–92.

Cavers, D. F. (1964), 'Improving financial protection of the public against the hazards of nuclear power', 77 *Harvard Law Review* 644, 1963–4.

Chandavarkar, A. (2009), *The Unexplored Keynes and Other Essays: A Socio-Economic Miscellany*, New Delhi, India: Academic Foundation.

Chanin, M. N. and Shapiro, H. J. (1985), 'Dialectical inquiry in strategic planning: extending the boundaries', *Academy of Management Review*, 10, 663–75.

Chapman, N. A. and McKinley, I. G. (1987), *The Geological Disposal of Nuclear Waste*, New York: Wiley.

Chu, S. (2010), Secretary of the US Department of Energy. Statement on the 4 February 2010 FY 2011 Budget Hearing before the Senate Committee on Energy and Natural Resources, available at http://energy.gov/sites/prod/files/ciprod/documents/2-4-10_Final_Testimony_(Chu).pdf (last accessed August 2011).

Clarke, L. (1985), 'The origins of nuclear power: a case of institutional conflict', *Social Problems*, 32 (5), 474–87.

Clarke, M. and Cummins, T. (2011), 'Judicial review in the energy sector: the England and Wales perspective', *International Energy Law Review*, 6, 244–52.

Climate Change Act 2008 chapter 27, London: The Stationery Office.

Coase, R. H. (1937), 'The nature of the firm', *Economica*, New Series, 4 (16), 386–405.

Commons Energy and Climate Change Committee (2011), 'Third Report on the "Revised Draft National Policy Statement on Energy"', *Journal of Planning and Environmental Law*, 394–7.

Conklin, J. (2003), Wicked Problems and Social Complexity. Working Paper, Cognexus Institute, 2001–2003, available at http://cognexus.org/wpf/wickedproblems.pdf] (last accessed January 2011).

Conservative Party (2010), Open Source Planning: Green Paper 2010 Policy Green Paper No. 14, available at http://www.conservatives.com/News/News_stories/2010/02/~/media/Files/Green%20Papers/planning-green-paper.ashx (last accessed December 2011).

Constantin, M. and Hristea, V. (2008), Nuclear Education and Information Technology in the 21st Century, Conference paper, Nuclear 2008, 28–30 May, Romania.

Corbey, D. (1995), 'Dialectical functionalism: stagnation as a booster of European integration', *International Organization*, 49 (2), 253–84.

Cosier, R. A. (1978), 'The effects of three potential aids for making strategic decisions on prediction accuracy', *Organizational Behavior and Human Performance*, 22, 295–306.

Cosier, R. A. (1980), 'Inquiry method, goal difficulty, and context effects on performance', *Decision Sciences*, 11, 1–16.

Cosier, R. A. (1981), 'Dialectical inquiry in strategic planning: a case of premature acceptance?', *Academy of Management Review*, 6, 643–8.

Cosier, R. A. and Aplin, J. C. (1980), 'A critical view of dialectical inquiry as a tool in strategic planning', *Strategic Management Journal*, 1, 343–56.

Cosier, R. A. and Rechner, P. L. (1985), 'Inquiry method effects on performance in a simulated business environment', *Organizational Behavior and Human Decision Processes*, 36, 79–95.

Cosier, R. A., Ruble, T. A. and Aplin, J. C. (1978), 'An evaluation of the effectiveness of dialectical inquiry systems', *Management Science*, 24, 1483–90.

Craciunoiu, C., Axworthy, M. W. A. and Scafes, C. (1995), *Third Axis Fourth Ally: Romanian Armed Forces in the European War, 1941–1945*, London: Arms and Armour.

Cullen, R. (1990), 'Report from Romania', *The New Yorker*, 2 April, 104.

Davies, D. (1984), 'The Sizewell B Nuclear Inquiry: an analysis of public participation in decision-making about nuclear power', *Science, Technology, and Human Values*, 9 (3), 21–32.

De Beaupuy, F. (2010), 'Areva Finnish nuclear plant overruns approach initial cost after provision', available at http://www.bloomberg.com/news/2010–06-24/areva-finnish-nuclear-plant-overruns-approach-initial-cost-after-provision.html (last accessed 10 November 2010).

Delmas, M. and Heiman, B. (2001), 'Government credible commitment to the French and American nuclear power industries', *Journal of Policy Analysis and Management*, 20 (3), 433–56.

Department for Business Enterprise and Regulatory Reform (BERR) (2008), Meeting the Energy Challenge: A White Paper on Nuclear Power, London: The Stationery Office.

Department for Communities and Local Government (2007), Planning for a Sustainable Future, White Paper, London: The Stationery Office.

Department of Energy and Climate Change (2009), Draft National Policy Statement for Nuclear Power Generation (EN-6), presented to Parliament pursuant to section 5(9b) of the Planning Act 2008, available at https://www.gov.uk/government/uploads/system/uploads/attachment_data/file/228630/9780108508332.pdf (last accessed March 2012).

Department of Energy and Climate Change (2011a), Planning Our Electric Future: A White Paper for Secure, Affordable and Low-carbon Electricity, London: The Stationery Office.

Department of Energy and Climate Change (2011b), Digest of United Kingdom Energy Statistics 2011, available at https://www.gov.uk/government/collections/digest-of-uk-energy-statistics-dukes (last accessed March 2012).

Department of Energy and Climate Change (2011c), UK Country Profile Analysis and Data, available at https://www.gov.uk/government/collections/digest-of-uk-energy-statistics-dukes (last accessed December 2011).

Department of Energy and Climate Change (2011d), UK Renewable Energy Roadmap, London: The Stationery Office.

Department of Energy and Climate Change (2012), Charles Hendry Comment on Horizon Nuclear Power, available at http://www.decc.gov.uk/en/content/cms/news/ch_horizon/ch_horizon.aspx (last accessed May 2012).

Department of Energy Organisation Act of 1977, Pub.L. 95–91, 91 Stat. 565.

Department of Trade and Industry (2002), Managing the Nuclear Legacy – A Strategy for Action, available at http://webarchive.national archives.gov.uk/+/http:/www.dti.gov.uk/nuclearcleanup/ach/white paper.pdf (last accessed May 2012).

Department of Trade and Industry (DTI) (2003), Energy White Paper: Our Energy Future – Creating a Low Carbon Economy, London: The Stationery Office.

Department of Trade and Industry (DTI) (2006), The Energy Challenge: Energy Review Report 2006, London: The Stationery Office.

Department of Trade and Industry (DTI) (2007), Meeting the Energy Challenge: White Paper on Energy 2007, London: The Stationery Office.

De Rond, M. and Bouchikhi, H. (2004), 'Dialectics of strategic alliances', Organization Science, 15 (1), 56–69.

De Roo, G. and Parsons, J. E. (2011), 'A methodology for calculating the levelized cost of electricity in nuclear power systems with fuel recycling', Energy Economics 33, 826–39.

Devine, F. (1995), 'Qualitative analysis', in Marsh, D. and Stoker, G. (eds), Theory and Methods in Political Science, London: Macmillan.

Diaconu, O., Oprescu, G. and Pittman, R. (2009), 'Electricity reform in Romania', Utilities Policy, 17 (1), 114–24.

Doherty, S. (2008), Heathrow's Terminal 5: History in the Making, Chichester: John Wiley and Sons.

Downward, P. and Mearman, A. (2007), 'Reintroduction as mixed methods triangulation in economics research: reorienting economics into social science', Cambridge Journal of Economics, 31 (1), 77–99.

Drobak, J. N. (1985), 'From turnpike to nuclear power: the constitutional limits on utility rate regulation', 65 Boston University Law Review 65.

Drolet, A. (2002), 'Inherent rule variability in consumer choice: changing rules for change's sake', The Journal of Consumer Research, 29 (3) 293–305.

Drottz-Sjoberg, B. and Sjoberg, L. (1990), 'Risk perception and worries after the Chernobyl accident', Journal of Environmental Psychology, 10, 135–49.

Dubin, J. A. and Rothwell, G. S. (1990), 'Subsidy to nuclear power through Price-Anderson liability limit', Contemporary Policy Issues, 8 (3), 73–9.

Eddington Transport Study (2006), Norwich: HMSO.

Energy Information Administration (EIA) (2010a), Executive Summary: Annual Energy Outlook 2010 with Projections to 2035, available at http://www.eia.gov/oiaf/aeo/pdf/execsummary.pdf (last accessed December 2010).

Energy Information Administration (EIA) (2010b), EIA Annual Energy Review 2009, available at ftp://ftp.eia.doe.gov/multifuel/038409.pdf (last accessed August 2011).

Energy Act 2008, chapter 32, London: The Stationery Office.

Energy Policy Act of 2005. Pub.L. 109–58.

Energy Reorganisation Act of 1974. Pub.L. 93–438, 88 Stat. 1223.

Europa (2005), C52/2003 Aid in Favour of British Energy Plc – Decision on 22 September 2004, available at http://ec.europa.eu/competition/elojade/isef/case_details.cfm?proc_code=3_C52_2003 (last accessed December 2011).

European Nuclear Energy Forum (2008), Subgroup 'Nuclear Legal Road Map' of Working Group 'Opportunities', 20 September 2008, available at http://ec.europa.eu/energy/nuclear/forum/opportunities/doc/legal_roadmap/the_importance_of_new_approaches_in_licensing.pdf, last accessed 1–15 May 2010.

Eurostat (2011), available at http://epp.eurostat.ec.europa.eu/portal/page/portal/statistics/search_database last accessed 1–15 February 2010.

Feinstein, J. S. (1989), 'The safety regulation of U.S. nuclear power plants: violations, inspections, and abnormal occurrences', *The Journal of Political Economy*, 97 (1), 115–54.

Ferlie, E., Lynn Jr, L. E. and Pollitt, C. (2005), *The Oxford Handbook of Public Management*, Oxford: Oxford University Press.

Financial Times (2012), 'Centrica concerned at State aid for N-plants', 27 May, available at http://www.ft.com/intl/cms/s/0/8b590ebe-a818-11e1-8fbb-00144feabdc0.html#axzz1y8HlnMxB (last accessed May 2012).

Flick, U. (2002), *An Introduction to Qualitative Research*, London: Sage.

Flyvbjerg, B. (2011), 'Managing major projects', in Morris, P. W. G., Pinto, J. K. and Soderlund, J. (eds), *The Oxford Handbook of Project Management*, Oxford: Oxford University Press.

Flyvbjerg, B., Bruzelius, N. and Rothengatter, W. (2003), *Megaprojects and Risk: An Anatomy of Ambition*, Cambridge: Cambridge University Press.

Flyvbjerg, B. and COWI (2004), Procedures for Dealing with Optimism Bias in Transport Planning: Guidance Document, London: Department for Transport.

Flyvbjerg, B., Garbuio, M. and Lovallo, D. (2009), 'Delusion and deception in large infrastructure projects: two models for explaining and preventing executive disaster', *California Management Review*, 51 (2), 170–93.

European Nuclear Energy Forum (2008), Subgroup 'Nuclear Legal Road Map' of Working Group 'Opportunities', 20 September 2008, available at http://ec.europa.eu/energy/nuclear/forum/opportunities/doc/legal_roadmap/the_importance_of_new_approaches_in_licensing.pdf (last accessed 1–15 May 2010).

Folkes, V. S., Martin, I. M. and Gupta, K. (1993), 'When to say when: effects of supply on usage', *The Journal of Consumer Research*, 20 (3), 467–77.

Froggatt, A., Thomas, S., Bradford, P. and Milborrow, D. (2007), *Economics of Nuclear Power in Europe*, London: Greenpeace Publishing.

Gamson, G. A. and Modigliani, A. (1989), 'Media discourse and public opinion on nuclear power: a constructionist approach', *The American Journal of Sociology*, 95 (1), 1–37.

Gallagher, T. (2009), *Romania and the European Union*, Manchester and New York: Palgrave Macmillan.

Ghiordanescu, N., Grecu, V. and Jipa, A. (2008), Nuclear Physics Education Today, Conference paper, Nuclear 2008, 28–30 May, Romania.

Giddens, A. (2009), *The Politics of Climate Change*, Cambridge: Polity Press.

Global Subsidies Initiative (2010), Relative Subsidies to Energy Sources, available at http://www.globalsubsidies.org/files/assets/relative_energy_subsidies.pdf (last accessed 1 May–20 July 2011).

Goodfellow, M. J., Williams, H. R. and Azapagic, A. (2011), 'Nuclear renaissance, public perception and design criteria: An exploratory review', *Energy Policy*, 39 (10), 6199–210.

Goodman, M. R. and Andes, F. P. (1985), 'The politics of regulatory reform and the future direction of nuclear energy policy', *Review of Policy Research*, 5 (1), 111–21.

Greenberg M. (2009), 'Energy sources, public policy, and public preferences: analysis of US national and site-specific data', *Energy Policy*, 37, 3242–9.

Greene, J. C., Caracelli, V. J. and Graham, W. F. (1989), 'Toward a conceptual framework for mixed method evaluation designs', *Educational Evaluation and Policy Analysis*, 11 (2), 255–74.

Grekos, M. (2010), 'Legislation and policy', *Environmental Law Review*, 12, 1 (50) 1 March.

Grimes, R. W. and Nuttall, W. J. (2010), 'Generating the option of a two-stage nuclear renaissance', *Science*, 329 (5993), 799–803.

Harding, J. (2007), 'Economics of nuclear power and proliferation risks in a carbon-constrained world', *Electricity Journal*, 20, 65–76.

Haye, H. (2012), keynote speaker at Nuclear Now, 23 February 2012, Commonwealth Club, London.

Hecht, G. (1998), *The Radiance of France: Nuclear Power and National Identity after World War II*, Cambridge, MA: The MIT Press.

Hecht, G. (2009), *The Radiance of France: Nuclear Power and National Identity after World War II*, 2nd edn, Cambridge, MA: The MIT Press.

Heffron, R. J. (2012), Nuclear New Build in the USA 1990–2010: A Three State Analysis. Electricity Policy Research Working Paper Series, EPRG WP 1204, Cambridge: University of Cambridge.

Heffron, R. J. (2012), 'Romanian nuclear new build: progress amidst turbulence', *Progress in Nuclear Energy*, 56, 43–60.

Helm, D. (2007), *The New Energy Paradigm*, Oxford: Oxford University Press.

Helman, H. B. (1968), 'Pre-emption: Approaching Federal-state conflict over licensing nuclear power plants', 51 *Marquette Law Review*, 43, 1967–8.

Hetherington, J. (1998), 'Nirex and deep disposal: the Cumbrian experience', in Barker, F. (ed.), *Management of Radioactive Wastes: Issues for Local Authorities*, London: Thomas Telford Publishing, pp. 17–32.

Higson, M. (2012), interview at Office for Nuclear Development, Department of Energy and Climate Change, London.

Hisschemoller, M. and Mol, A. P. J. (eds) (2002), *Climate Options for the Long Term (COOL). Evaluating the Dialogues. Final Report - Volume E.* Bilthoven, Netherlands: NRP report 410 200 119.

HM Government, The UK Low Carbon Transition Plan: National Strategy for Climate and Energy, available at https://www.gov.uk/government/uploads/system/uploads/attachment_data/file/228752/97801085 08394.pdf (last accessed 12 May 2011).

Hohenemser, C., Kasperson, R. and Kates, R. W. (1977), 'The distrust of nuclear power', *Science*, 196, 25–43.

Holmes, S. (1996), 'Cultural legacies or state collapse? Probing the postcommunist dilemma', in Mandelbaum, M. (ed.), *1996. Post-Communism: Four Perspectives*, New York: Council on Foreign Relations.

Holt, M. (2011), Nuclear Energy Policy, Congressional Research Service, available at http://energy.gov/sites/prod/files/ciprod/documents/2-4-10_Final_Testimony_(Chu).pdf (last accessed 6 February 2012).

Hultman, N. E. (2011), 'The political economy of nuclear energy', *WIREs Climate Change* 2 397–411.

IAEA (International Atomic Energy Agency) (2007), Milestones in the Development of a National Infrastructure for Nuclear Power. No. NG-G-3.1, Vienna, Austria: IAEA Publishing, available at http://www-pub.iaea.org/MTCD/publications/PDF/Pub1305_web.pdf (last accessed September 2011).

IAEA (International Atomic Energy Agency) (2008), Competitiveness of Nuclear Energy: IAEA's Perspective and Study Results for Europe.

Report by Sokolov, Y. A., Deputy Director General, IAEA, November 2008, Vienna, Austria: IAEA Publishing.

IAEA, (2010), International Status and Prospects of Nuclear Power, available at http://www.iaea.org/Publications/Booklets/NuclearPower/np10.pdf (last accessed 1–15 May 2010).

IEA, OPEC, OECD and World Bank Joint Report (2010), Analysis of the Scope of Energy Subsidies and Suggestions for the G-20 Initiative, available at http://www.iea.org/weo/docs/G20_Subsidy_Joint_Report.pdf (last accessed 1 May–20 July 2011.

Illie, Liae, Horobet, A. and Popescu, C. (2007), Liberalisation and Regulation in the EU Energy Market. MPRA Paper No. 6419, University Library of Munich, Germany, available at http://mpra.ub.uni-muenchen.de/6419/ (last accessed 10–25 January 2010).

Independent Planning Commission (IPC), (2012), National Infrastructure Planning: Hinkley Point C New Nuclear Power Station, available at http://infrastructure.independent.gov.uk/projects/south-west/hinkley-point-c-new-nuclear-power-station/ (last accessed December 2011).

Jann, W. (1997), 'Public management reform in Germany: a revolution without theory?', in Kickert, W. J. M. (ed.), *Public Management And Administrative Reform in Western Europe*, Cheltenham: Edward Elgar, pp. 81–100.

Jasper, J. M. (1990), *Nuclear Politics: Energy and the State in the United States, Sweden, and France*, Princeton: Princeton University Press.

Joppke, C. (1991), 'Social movements during cycles of issue attention: the decline of the anti-nuclear energy movements in West Germany and the USA', *The British Journal of Sociology*, 42 (1), 43–60.

Jora, S. (2006), 'European Integration and Democratic Consolidation in Romania Towards a Universal Modus Operandi?', The Sphere of Politics, 125/2006, available at http://sferapoliticii.ro/sfera/pdf/Sfera_125.pdf#page=66 (last accessed 5 August 2014).

Joskow, P. L. (1997), 'Restructuring, competition, and regulatory reform in the US electricity sector', *Journal of Economic Perspectives*, 11 (3), 119–38.

Joskow, P. L. (2005), Markets for Power in the United States: An Interim Assessment. Working Paper 05–20 September 2005, AEI-Brookings Joint Center for Regulatory Studies, available at http://ssrn.com/abstract= 845785 or www.aei-brookings.org (last accessed August 2010).

Joskow, P. L. (2006), The Future of Nuclear Power in the United States: Economic and Regulatory Challenges. Report by the Joint Center of the Department of Economics, Laboratory for Energy and the Environment, and the Sloan School of Management, December 2006, Massachusetts: MIT.

Joskow, P. L. and Baughman, M. L. (1976), 'The future of the US nuclear energy industry', *The Bell Journal of Economics*, 7 (1), 3–32.

Kahneman, D. (1994), 'New challenges to the rationality assumption', *Journal of Institutional and Theoretical Economics* 150, 18–36.

Kahneman, D. and Tversky, A. (1979), 'Prospect theory: an analysis of decisions under risk', *Econometrica*, 47, 313–27.

Kasperson, R. E., Berk, G., Pijawka, D., Sharaf, A.B. and Wood, J. (1980), 'Public opposition to nuclear energy: retrospect and prospect', *Science, Technology, and Human Values*, 5 (31), 11–23.

Keating, M. (2010), *The Government of Scotland: Public Policy Making After Devolution*, 2nd edn, Edinburgh: Edinburgh University Press.

Keay, M. (2007), Energy: The Long View. Working Paper SP20, Oxford: Oxford Institute for Energy Studies.

Kennedy, D. (2007), 'New nuclear power generation in the UK: cost benefit analysis', *Energy Policy*, 35, 3701–16.

Kincaid, J. (1990), 'From cooperative to coercive federalism', *Annals of the American Academy of Political and Social Science*, 509, 139–52.

Kincaid, J. and Cole, R. L. (2005), 'Public opinion on issues of US federalism in 2005: end of the post-2001 pro-federal surge?', *Publius*, 35 (1) 169–85.

Kitschelt, H. P. (1982), 'Structures and sequences of nuclear energy policy-making: suggestions for a comparative perspective', *Political Power and Social Theory* 3, 271–308.

Kitschelt, H. P. (1986), 'Political opportunity structures and political protest: anti-nuclear movements in four democracies', *British Journal of Political Science*, 16, 57–85.

Komanoff, C. (1981), *Power Plant Cost Escalation*, New York: Van Nostrand Reinhold.

Kriesi H. and Jegen, M. (2001), 'The Swiss energy policy elite: the actor constellation of a policy domain in transition', *European Journal of Political Research*, 39 (2) 251–87.

Kuklinski, J. H., Metlay, D. S. and Kay, W. D. (1982), 'Citizen knowledge and choices on the complex issue of nuclear energy', *American Journal of Political Science*, 26 (4), 615–42.

Lawson, T. (1997), *Economics and Reality*, London: Routledge.

Lawson, T. (2003), *Reorienting Economics*, London: Routledge.

Lawson, T. (2009), 'Applied economics, contrast explanation and asymmetric information', *Cambridge Journal of Economics*, 33, 405–19.

Lester, R. (1986), 'Rethinking nuclear power', *Scientific American*, 254, 31–9, March.

Light, D. (2006), 'Modern Romania: an historical overview', in Phinnemore, D., *The EU and Romania: Accession and Beyond*, London: The Federal Trust.

Light, D. and Phinnemore, D. (2001), *Post-Communist Romania: Coming to Terms with Transition*, Basingstoke: Palgrave.

Lilleker, D.G. (2003), 'Interviewing the political elite: navigating a potential minefield', *Politics*, 23 (3) 207–14.

Little, G. (2000), 'Scottish devolution and environmental law', *Journal of Environmental Law*, 12 (2), 155–74.

Lourenco, S. V. and Glidewell, J. C. (1975), 'A dialectical analysis of organizational conflict', *Administrative Science Quarterly*, 20 (4), 489–508.

Lund, P. (2006), 'Market penetration rates of new energy technologies', *Energy Policy*, 34 (17), 3317–26.

Lutz, D. S. (1992), 'The state constitutional pedigree of the US Bill of Rights', *Publius*, 22 (2) 19–45.

Lynn Jr, L. E. (2005), 'Public management: a concise history of the field', in Ferlie, E., Lynn Jr, L. E. and Pollitt, C. (eds), *The Oxford Handbook of Public Management*, Oxford: Oxford University Press.

MacKay, D. J. C. (2009), *Sustainable Energy: Without the Hot Air*, Cambridge: UIT Press.

MacKerron, G. (2004), 'Nuclear power and the characteristics of "ordinariness" – the case of UK energy policy', *Energy Policy*, 32 (17), 1957–65.

Maleson, D. C. (1982), 'The historical roots of the legal system's response to nuclear power', 55 *Southern California Law Review* 597, 1981–2.

Mason, R. O. (1969), 'A dialectical approach to strategic planning', *Management Science*, 15, B403–B414.

Mason, R. O. and Mitroff, I. I. (1981), *Challenging Strategic Planning Assumptions: Theory, Cases and Techniques*, New York: Wiley.

Massachusetts v Environmental Protection Agency, 549 U. S. 497 (2007).

Massachusetts Institute of Technology (MIT) (2003), The Future of Nuclear Power: An Interdisciplinary Study, available at http://web.mit.edu/nuclearpower/ (last accessed December 2010).

Massachusetts Institute of Technology (MIT) (2009), Update of the MIT 2003 Future of Nuclear Power: An Interdisciplinary Study, available at http://web.mit.edu/nuclearpower/ (last accessed December 2010).

Matisoff, D. C. (2008), 'The adoption of state climate change policies and renewable portfolio standards: regional diffusion or internal determinants', *Review of Policy Research*, 25 (6), 527–46.

Maugis, V. and Nuttall, W. J. (2008), Metapolicy Options for Energy in England. EPRG Working Paper 0818, Cambridge: University of Cambridge.

Miles, M. B. and Huberman, A. M. (1994), *Qualitative Data Analysis*, London: Sage.

Mitroff, I. I. (1971), 'A communication model of dialectical inquiring systems – a strategy for strategic planning', *Management Science*, 17 (10), B634-B648.

Mitroff, I. I., Barabba, V. P. and Kilmann, R. H. (1977), 'The application of behavioral and philosophical technologies to strategic planning: a case study of a large federal agency', *Management Science*, 24, 44–58.

Mitroff, I. I. and Mason, R. O. (1981), 'The metaphysics of policy and planning: a reply to Cosier', *Academy of Management Review*, 6, 649–52.

Moore, R. C. (2011), Enhancing the Role of the State and Local Governments in America's Nuclear Future: An Idea Whose Time Has Come. Prepared for the Blue Ribbon Commission, Clancy, MT: Pronghorn Engineering.

Mooz, W. E. (1978), Cost Analysis of Light Water Reactor Power Plants. R-2304-DOE, Santa Monica, CA: Rand Corporation.

Mooz, W. E. (1979), A Second Cost Analysis of Light Water Reactor Power Plants. R-1899-DOE, Santa Monica, CA: Rand Corporation.

Morone J. G. and Woodhouse, E. J. (1989), *The Demise of Nuclear Energy? Lessons for Democratic Control of Technology*, New Haven, CT: Yale University Press.

Morris, P. W. G., Pinto, J. K. and Soderlund, J. (2011), 'Towards the third wave of project management', in Morris, P. W. G., Pinto, J. K. and Soderlund, J. (eds), *The Oxford Handbook of Project Management*, Oxford: Oxford University Press.

Moss, T. and Sills, D. (1981), *The Three Mile Island Nuclear Accident*, New York: New York Academy of Sciences.

Mullin, M. and Daley D. M. (2009), 'Working with the state: exploring interagency collaboration within a federalist system', *Journal of Public Administration Research*, 20, 757–78.

Nagao, D. H. and Davis, J. H. (1980), 'The effects of prior experience on mock juror case judgments', *Social Psychology Quarterly*, 43 (2), 190–9.

National Commission, (2011), Deep Water: The Gulf Oil Disaster and the Future of Offshore Drilling. Report to the President. National Commission on the BP Deepwater Horizon Oil Spill and Offshore Drilling, available at http://www.oilspillcommission.gov/sites/default/files/documents/DEEPWATER_ReporttothePresident_FINAL.pdf, last accessed December 2011.

NATO (2011), NATO History, available at http://www.nato.int/history/nato-history.html (last accessed December 2011).

Navarro, P. (1988), 'Comparative energy policy: the economics of nuclear power in Japan and the US', *Energy Journal*, 9 (4) 1–16.

NEA, (1995), Chernobyl Accident, Paris: OECD NEA Publishing; also available at http://www.nea.fr/rp/chernobyl/chernobyl-1995.pdf, last accessed 10–25 January 2010.

Nelkin, D. (1981), 'Some social and political dimensions of nuclear power: examples from Three Mile Island', *The American Political Science Review*, 75 (1), 132–42.

Nelkin, D. (1995), *Selling Science: How the Press Covers Science and Technology*, New York: W. H. Freeman.

New York Times (1987), 'Chernobyl officials are sentenced to labor camp', 30 July 1987, available at www.nytimes.com/1987/07/30/world/chernobyl-officials-are-sentenced-to-labor-camp.html?pagewanted=1 (last accessed 1–15 February 2009).

Nohrstedt, D. (2005), 'External shocks and policy change: Three Mile Island and Swedish nuclear energy policy', *Journal of European Public Policy*, 12 (6), 1041–59.

Nohrstedt, D. (2008), 'The politics of crisis policy-making: Chernobyl and Swedish nuclear energy policy', *The Policy Studies Journal*, 36 (2), 257–78.

Nohrstedt, D. (2009), 'Do advocacy coalitions matter? Crisis and change in Swedish nuclear energy policy', *Journal of Public Administration Research and Theory*, 20, 309–33.

Nuclear Engineering International (NEI) (2012), 'EDF plans longer life extensions for UK AGRs', 20 February 2012, available at http://www.neimagazine.com/story.asp?sc=2061782 (last accessed February 2012).

Nuclear Industry Association (NIA) (2011), UK Country Profile Analysis and Data, at www.niauk.org (last accessed December 2011).

Nuclear Information Project (2005), Romania's Special Weapons, available at http://www.fas.org/nuke/guide/romania/index.html (accessed 15 February 2009).

Nuclear Regulatory Commission (NRC) (2007), Reactor License Renewal Overview, available at www.nrc.gov/reactors/operating/licensing/renewal/overview.html (last accessed August 2011).

Nuclear Regulatory Commission (NRC) (2008), Yucca Mountain Licence Application, available at http://www.nrc.gov/waste/hlw-disposal/yucca-lic-app.html (last accessed August 2011).

Nuclear Regulatory Commission (NRC) (2010), Nuclear Reactor License Renewal, available at http://www.nrc.gov/reactors/operating/licensing/renewal.html (last accessed at August 2011).

Nuclear Regulatory Commission (NRC), (2010), US Commercial Nuclear Power Reactors – Years of Operation, available at http://www.nrc.gov/reactors/operating/map-power-reactors.html (last accessed August 2011).

Nuclear Regulatory Commission (NRC) (2011), Statistics on Licence Renewals and Power Upgrades, available at http://www.nrc.gov/reactors/operating/licensing/renewal/applications.html; http://www.nrc.gov/reading-rm/doc-collections/fact-sheets/power-uprates.html (last accessed August 2011).

Nuttall, W. J. (2005), *Nuclear Renaissance: Technologies and Policies for the Future of Nuclear Power*, Bristol and Philadelphia: Institute of Physics Publishing.

Nuttall, W. J. (2010). Nuclear energy in the enlarged European Union', in Leveque, F., Glachant, J., Barquin, J., Von Hirschhauen, C., Holz, F. and Nuttall, W. (eds), *Security of Energy Supply in Europe: Natural Gas, Nuclear and Hydrogen*, Cheltenham: Edward Elgar.

Nuttall, W. J. and Taylor, S. (2009), 'Financing the nuclear renaissance', *European Review of Energy Markets*, 3 (2), 187–202.

Obama, B. (2010), 17 February Announcement of $48.3 billion Federal Loan Guarantee, available online http://abcnews.go.com/blogs/politics/2010/02/obama-says-safe-nuclear-power-plants-are-a-necessary-investment/ (last accessed August 2011).

OFGEM (2011), The Retail Market Review: Findings and Initial Proposals; OFGEM, 21 March. Press release: 'Supply companies failing consumers: OFGEM proposes radical overhaul', available at https://www.ofgem.gov.uk/ofgem-publications/76316/rmrfinal-final.pdf (last accessed August 2012).

Olson, M. (1971), *The Logic of Collective Action: Public Goods and the Theory of Groups*, Cambridge, MA: Harvard University Press.

Paik, S. and Schriver, W. (1979), 'The effect of increased regulation on capital costs and manual labor requirements of nuclear power', *The Engineering Economist*, 26 (3), 223–44.

Palfreman, J. (2006), 'A tale of two fears: exploring media depictions of nuclear power and global warming', *Review of Policy Research*, 23, (1), 23–43.

Parenteau, P. A. (1976), 'Regulation of nuclear power plants: A constitutional dilemma for the States', 6 *Environmental Law* 675, 1975–6.

Pepitone, A. and M. DeNubile. (1976), 'Contrast effects in judgments of crime severity and the punishment of criminal violators', *Journal of Personality and Social Psychology*, 33, 448–59.

Perin, C. (2005), *Shouldering Risks. The Culture of Control in the Nuclear Power Industry*. Princeton: Princeton University Press.

Petra, N, M., Maria, I., Mirela, D., Bogdan, B. I. and Ileana (2008), The Role of Research Programs and Commercial Contracts for Increase of Economic Competitiveness and Development at INR Pitesti, Conference paper, Nuclear 2008, 28–30 May, Romania.

Pidgeon, N. F., Lorenzoni, I. and Poortinga, W. (2008), 'Climate change or nuclear power – no thanks! A quantitative study of public perceptions and risk framing in Britain', *Global Environmental Change* 18 (2008) 69–85.

Pinkstone, B. (2002), 'Persistent demi-regs and robust tendencies: critical realism and the Singer-Prebisch thesis', *Cambridge Journal of Economics*, 36, 561–83.

Planning Act, 2008 chapter 29, London: The Stationery Office.

Planning for a Sustainable Future, White Paper, (2007), Department of Communities and Local Government, London: The Stationery Office.

Planning Our Electric Future: A White Paper for Secure, Affordable and Low-carbon Electricity (2011), Department of Energy and Climate Change, London: The Stationery Office.

Plantanol GmbH v Hauptzollamt Barmstadt (C-201/08) [2009] ECR I-08343.

Plato (1975), *The Laws of Plato* (with an introduction by Trevor J. Saunders), Harmondsworth: Penguin.

Plushnick-Masti, R. (2011), 'Commission lets 36 states dump nuclear waste in Texas', available at http://www.huffingtonpost.com/2011/01/05/commission-36-states-nuclear-waste-texas_n_804527.html (last accessed December 2011).

Pollitt, M. (2009), 'Evaluating the evidence on electricity reform: lessons for the South East Europe (SEE) market', *Utilities Policy*, 17 (1), 13–23.

Pope, D. (2008), *Nuclear Implosions: The Rise and Fall of the Washington Public Power Supply System*, Cambridge: Cambridge University Press.

Pratten, S. (2004), 'Mathematical formalism in economics: consequences and alternatives', *Economic Affairs*, 24 (2), 37–42.

Pratten, S. (2007), 'Realism, closed systems and abstraction', *Journal of Economic Methodology*, 14 (4), 473–497.

Prodea, I., Margeanu, C. A., Prisecaru, I., Danila, N. and Aioanei, C. (2008), Nuclear Electricity Share Growing – a key factor for sustainable energetic development of Romania in the next decades. Conference Paper, Nuclear 2008, 28– 30 May, Romania.

Proops, J. (2001), 'The (non-) economics of the nuclear fuel cycle: an historical and discourse analysis', *Ecological Economics*, 39, 13–19.

Raadschelders, J. C. N. and Rutgers, M.R. (1999), 'The waxing and waning of the state and its study: changes and challenges in the study of public administration', in Kickert, W. J. M. and Stillman II, R. J. (eds), *The Modern State and its Study: New Administrative Sciences in a Changing Europe and United States*, Cheltenham: Edward Elgar, pp. 17–35.

Rabe, B. G. (2004), *Statehouse and Greenhouse: The Emerging Politics Of American Climate Change Policy*, Washington, DC: Brookings Institution.

Rabe, B.G. (2006), *Race to the Top: The Expanding Role of US State Renewable Portfolio Standards*, Arlington, VA: Pew Center on Global Climate Change.

Rabe, B. G. (2007), 'Environmental policy and the Bush era: the collision between the administrative presidency and state experimentation', *Publicus: The Journal of Federalism*, 37 (3), 413–31.

Rabe, B. G. (2008), 'States on steroids: The intergovernmental odyssey of American climate policy', *Review of Policy Research*, 25 (2), 105–28.

Robbins, J. (1997), 'Lessons from Chernobyl: the event, the aftermath fallout: radioactive, political, social. *Thyroid*, 7 (2), 189–92.

Robinson, P. (2009), 'Energy planning in 2009, all systems go?', *Journal of Planning and Environmental Law*, 13, (53).

Romania Statistical Yearbook 2009, Bucharest: National Institute of Statistics.

Romanian Daily (2006), 'State subsidies for nuclear and naval shipyards', 21 April, available at http://romaniandaily.ro/site_archives/April2006_html (last accessed 1–15 February 2009).

Rosa, E. A. and Dunlap, R. E. (1994), 'The polls – poll trends. Nuclear power: three decades of public opinion', *Public Opinion Quarterly*, vol. 38, 295–325.

Ross, W. T. and Simonson, I. (1991), 'Evaluations of pairs of experiences: a preference for happy endings', *Journal of Behavioural Decision Making*, 4 (4), 273–82.

Rossin, A. D. and Rieck, T. A. (1978), 'Economics of nuclear power', *Science*, New Series, 201 (4356), 582–9.

Rothman, S. and Lichter, S. R. (1987), 'Elite ideology and risk perception in nuclear energy policy', *The American Political Science Review*, 81 (2), 383–404.

Royal Academy of Engineering, (2010), *Nuclear Lessons Learnt*, London: RAE.

Sailor, W. C., Bodansky, D., Braun, C., Fetter, S. and Van der Zwaan, B. (2000), 'Nuclear power: a nuclear solution to climate change?' *Science*, 288 (5469), 1177.

Samuels, W. J. (1971), 'Interrelations between legal and economic processes', *Journal of Law and Economics*, 14, 435–50.

Schechter, D. (2011), 'West Texas facility ready for nuclear waste', available at http://www.wfaa.com/news/texas-news/West-Texas-facility-ready-for-nuclear-waste-115543929.html (last accessed December 2011).

Schweiger, D. M. and Finger, P. A. (1984), 'The comparative effectiveness of dialectical inquiry and devil's advocacy: the impact of task biases on previous research findings', *Strategic Management Journal*, 5 (4), 335–50.

Schweiger, D. M., Sandberg, W. R. and Ragan, J. W. (1986), 'Group approaches for improving strategic decision making: a comparative analysis of dialectical inquiry, devil's advocacy, and consensus', *Academy of Management Journal*, 29, 51–71.

Schwenk, C. R. (1982a), 'Dialectical inquiry in strategic decision making: a comment on the continuing debate', *Strategic Management Journal*, 3, 371–3.

Schwenk, C. R. (1982), 'Why sacrifice rigour for relevance? A proposal for combining laboratory and field research in strategic management', *Strategic Management Journal*, 3, 213–25.

Schwenk, C. R. and Cosier, R. A. (1980), 'Effects of the expert, devil's advocate, and dialectical inquiry methods on prediction performance', *Organizational Behavioral and Human Performance*, 26, 409–24.

Scottish Government (2008), Energy Policy: An Overview, available at http://www.scotland.gov.uk/Resource/Doc/237670/0065265.pdf (last accessed December 2013).

Select Committee on Trade and Industry (SCTI) (1998), Fourth Report, April 7, 1998, section III, para. 38, available at http://www.publications.parliament.uk/pa/cm199798/cmselect/cmtrdind/659s4/tis402. htm (last accessed December 2013).

Seo, M. and Creed, W. E. D. (2002), 'Institutional contradictions, praxis, and institutional change: a dialectical perspective', *Academy of Management Review*, 27, 222–47.

Sherif, M. and Hovland, C. I. (1961), *Social Judgment: Assimilation and Contrast Effects in Communication and Attitude Change*, New Haven, CT: Yale University Press.

Slocum, T. (2008), The Failure of Electricity Deregulation: History, Status, and Needed Reforms. Public Citizen's Energy Program, available at www.citizen.org (last accessed August 2010).

Soderlund, J. (2011), 'Theoretical foundations of project management: suggestions for a pluralistic understanding', in Morris, P. W. G., Pinto, J. K. and Soderlund, J. (eds), *The Oxford Handbook of Project Management*, Oxford: Oxford University Press.

Sovacool, B. K. (2008), 'The costs of failure: a preliminary assessment of major accidents, 1907–2007', *Energy Policy*, vol. 36, no. 5.

Stefan, A. M. (2009), *Democratization and Securitization: The Case of Romania*, Leiden: Brill.

Stevens, P. (2007), 'Oil markets and the future', in Helm, D. (ed.), *The New Energy Paradigm*, Oxford: Oxford University Press.

Stoiber, C., Baer, A., Pelzer, N. and Tonhauser, W. (2003), *Handbook of Nuclear Law*, Vienna: International Atomic Energy Agency.

Stoler, P. (1985), *Decline and Fall: The Ailing Nuclear Power Industry*, New York: Dodd, Mead and Company.

Taylor, F. W. (1911), *The Principles of Scientific Management*, New York: Harper.

Taylor, F. W. (1916), 'Government efficiency', *Bulletin of the Taylor Society*, December 191, 7–13.

Taylor, S. (2007), *Privatization and Financial Collapse in the Nuclear Industry – the Origins and Cause of the British Energy Crisis of 2002*, London: Routledge.

Taylor, S. (2011), Can New Nuclear Power Plants be Project Financed?, Cambridge Working Paper in Economics 1140, Cambridge: University of Cambridge.

Temples, J. R. (1980), 'The politics of nuclear power: a subgovernment in transition', *Political Science Quarterly*, 95 (2), 239–60.

Texas Comptroller of Public Accounts (2008), 'Energy Report 2008', available at http://www.window.state.tx.us/specialrpt/energy/ (last accessed August 2011).

Texas Comptroller of Public Accounts (2010), 'A Review of the Texas Economy: Federal Deficits and the National Debt', available at http://www.window.state.tx.us/specialrpt/energy/ (last accessed August 2011).

The Nuclear Information Project (2005), Romania's Special Weapons, available at http://www.fas.org/nuke/guide/romania/index.html (last accessed 1–15 February 2009).

Thomas, S. (2010), 'Competitive energy markets and nuclear power: can we have both, do we want either?', Energy Policy, 38, 4903–8.

Timney, M. M. (2002), 'Short circuit: Federal-state relations in the California energy crisis', Publius, 32 (4) 109–22.

Tolnay, Adam (2002), Ceauşescu's Journey to the East, The 4th Annual Kokkalis Graduate Student Workshop, Kennedy School of Government, Harvard University, February 2002, available at http://www.hks.harvard.edu/kokkalis/GSW4/TolnayPAPER.PDF (last accessed 5–25 August 2009).

Tomei, J., Lucas, K. and Vanner, R. (2006), Citizen Science for Sustainability (SuScit), Policy Studies Institute and Centre for Sustainable Development (University of Westminister) Joint EPSRC project, United Kingdom.

Tonhauser, W. and Wetherall, A. (2010), 'The international legal framework on nuclear safety: developments, challenges and opportunities', in International Nuclear Law: History, Evolution and Outlook, Paris: OECD Nuclear Energy Agency.

Traicu, R. (2008), Perspectives and Constraints in Romanian Energy, Romania: RAAN – Romanian Authority for Nuclear Activities.

Turner, A. (2010), Economics, Conventional Wisdom and Public Policy. Presented at the Institute for New Economic Thinking Conference at King's College, Cambridge, UK, 8–11 April 2010.

Turnock, D. (2007), Aspects of Romania's Economic History with Particular Reference to Transition for EU Accession, Aldershot: Ashgate Publishing.

Tweena, M. (2006), Nuclear Energy: Rise, Fall and Resurrection, Cicero Working Paper 2006:01, Norway, available at http://www.cicero.uio.no/media/4101.pdf (last accessed 5–25 August 2009).

United Nations (2006), Romania's experience on the relationship between the competition authority and the sector regulators. Submitted to

UNCTAD's Seventh Session of the Intergovernmental Group of Experts on Competition Law and Policy, Geneva, 30 October-2 November 2006, available at http://www.unctad.org/sections/wcmu/docs/c2clp_ige7p6_en.pdf (last accessed 5–25 August 2009).

US EIA, (2010), Annual Energy Outlook 2010 with Projections to 2035. US Nuclear Power Plants: Continued life or replacement after 60. Available at http://www.eia.gov/oiaf/aeo/otheranalysis/aeo_2010 analysispapers/nuclear_power.html (last accessed December 2010).

US EPA (Environmental Protection Agency) (2011), US EPA Expert Elicitation Task Force White Paper, available at http://www.epa.gov/stpc/pdfs/ee-white-paper-final.pdf. Previous 2009 draft version available at http://www.epa.gov/osa/pdfs/elicitation/Expert_Elicitation_White_Paper-January_06_2009.pdf (last acceessed December 2013).

Van de Kerkhof, M. (2006), 'Making a difference: on the constraints of consensus building and the relevance of deliberation in stakeholder dialogues', *Policy Sciences*, 39 (3), 279–99.

Van Norrden, R. (2010), 'Carbon sequestration: buried trouble', *Nature*, 463, 871–3.

Wachs, M. (1986), 'Technique vs advocacy in forecasting: a study of rail rapid transit', *Urban Resources*, 4 (1), 23–30.

Wachs, M. (1990), 'Ethics and advocacy in forecasting for public policy', *Business and Professional Ethics Journal*, 9 (1–2), 141–57.

Wallace, M. J. (2010), Letter from Michael J. Wallace, Vice Chairman and Chief Operating Officer, Constellation Energy, to Dan Poneman, Deputy Secretary of Energy, 8 October 2010, available at http://media.washingtonpost.com/wp-srv/hp/ssi/wpc/constellationenergy.PDF?sid=ST2010100900005 (last accessed October 2011).

Waltz, K, N. (1990), 'Nuclear myths and political realities', *The American Political Science Review*, 84 (3), 731–45.

Watson, J. and Scott, A. (2009), 'New nuclear power in the UK: a strategy for energy security?', *Energy Policy*, 37, 5094–104.

Weinberg, A. M. (1972), 'Social institutions and nuclear energy', *Science*, New Series, 177 (4043), 27–34.

Wison, C. A. (2000), 'Policy regimes and policy change', *Journal of Public Policy*, vol. 20, Cambridge University Press.

Wolak, F. A. (2000), *Report on Electricity Industry Restructuring in Romania*, Palo Alto, CA: Stanford University Press.

World Nuclear Association (2010), World Nuclear Power Reactors, available at http://www.world-nuclear.org/info/reactors.html (last accessed December 2011).

Wynne, B. (1982), *Rationality and Ritual: The Windscale Inquiry and Nuclear Decisions in Britain*, Chalfont St Giles: British Society for the History of Science.

Yellin, J. (1981), 'High technology and the courts: nuclear power and the need for institutional reform', *Harvard Law Review*, 94 (3), 489–560.

Zimmerman, J. F. (1990), 'Regulating intergovernmental relations in the 1990s', *Annals of the American Academy of Political and Social Science*, 509, 48–59.

Zimmerman, M. B. (1982), 'Learning effects and the commercialization of new energy technologies: the case of nuclear power', *The Bell Journal of Economics*, 13 (2), 297–310.

Index